D1145270

80

AN ILLUSTRATED GUIDE TO
HORSE
AND PONY CARE

A comprehensive guide to riding, schooling and caring for your horse

AN ILLUSTRATED GUIDE TO
HORSE
AND PONY CARE

A comprehensive guide to riding, schooling and caring for your horse

Compiled by
Jane Kidd

a Salamander book

Published by Salamander Books Limited
LONDON

A Salamander Book

© 1981 Salamander Books Ltd.,
Salamander House,
27 Old Gloucester Street,
London WC1N 3AF,
United Kingdom.

ISBN 0 86101 091 4

Distributed in the United Kingdom
by New English Library Ltd.

All rights reserved. No part of this
book may be reproduced, stored in a
retrieval system or transmitted in any
form or by any means, electronic,
mechanical, photocopying, recording
or otherwise, without the prior
permission of Salamander Books Ltd.

All correspondence concerning the
content of this volume should be
addressed to Salamander Books Ltd.

Publisher's note: This book is based
upon the material appearing in *The
Horse and Pony Manual.*

Contents

Credits

Jane Kidd is well versed in equestrian topics; having competed successfully in international show-jumping events, Jane now concentrates on dressage, organizing events, competing and judging. In addition to writing for books and magazines, Jane helps to run the family stud. She particularly enjoys helping other riders and training horses.

Editors: Geoff Rogers, Marita Westberg
Designer: Nick Buzzard
Copy-editor: Maureen Cartwright
Line drawings: Glenn Steward
(John Martin & Artists Ltd.)
© Salamander Books Ltd.
Photographs: A full list of credits is given on page 200.
Colour/monochrome reproductions: Metric Reproductions Ltd., Essex, UK. Bantam Litho Ltd., Essex, UK.
Filmset: Modern Text Typesetting Ltd., Essex, United Kingdom.

Printed in Belgium by
Henri Proost et Cie, Turnhout.

Learning to Ride

In recent years 'horse-fever' has become almost an epidemic in the Western world. No one is exempt and few ever recover once the contact is made. Why this should be so is hard to say—perhaps because the horse can be all things to all men; because riding is a shared adventure; because the horse's speed and agility, which so exceeds that of man, can for a short while be his; and because horses have such courage and gentleness. Sadly the love and use of horses is not always to their benefit. Ignorance of the right way to care for horses can lead to unconscious cruelty.

HOW TO LEARN

The first stages

Much thoughtlessness can be avoided if newcomers are carefully instructed. The novice should start his riding career at a good riding school where he knows he will be safely mounted on horses suited to his ability. A few weeks' tuition at such an establishment, learning the basic seat and becoming familiar with the use of the aids, will pay dividends in the future.

Riding is rated a high-risk sport, and the figures for riders and animals killed—especially on the roads—grow yearly. For this reason alone, it is not enough to get a few lessons from 'that nice young girl down the road', who may know very little more than her pupil. Always seek expert tuition.

A good school will always be willing to advise beginners on what to wear and will insist that its pupils always ride in a hard hat. Strong shoes or boots with a full-

Below: This rider is badly dressed. The hat is too big and will come off in a fall. Wrinkled jeans will rub and bare legs may get pinched during riding. The shoes are too large and the rubber soles will easily catch in the stirrup.

length sole and a low heel are also essential, and for comfort and looks either jodhpurs or breeches and a hacking jacket or polo-neck sweater should be worn. Jeans or loose trousers tend to make the rider's seat unstable and provide less protection from saddle-sores than breeches.

Another good reason for starting a riding career at a school is that faults in the rider's position will be corrected before they become

Left top: Learning to ride on the lunge enables riders to forget about controlling the horse and concentrate on their position. Until confident and balanced it is wise to keep hold of the pommel. When the rider finds it natural to sit in the correct position and is relaxed enough to follow the pony's movement without bouncing around then she can take her hands off the pommel.
Left centre: In this exercise the rider swings the upper body and arms first to one side and then the other. This helps to make the hips and small of the back more supple.
Left bottom: Keeping the arms horizontal to the ground and swinging them backwards and forwards is good for the shoulders.
Below: The boy on the pony is too close to the horse in front; there should be at least one length between the horses.

established. It may also save the older rider from the painful back conditions that can spring from faulty posture. With a secure position in the saddle, a rider will gain confidence and will be able to use his reins to guide and control his horse rather than as a means of maintaining his own balance. He will learn to ride correctly over jumps instead of relying on the courage and speed of his horse to get him to the other side. For full advice on jumping see pages 24-25.

Owning a horse

Not until a rider is reasonably proficient should he think of acquiring his own horse. By then he should have ridden many different ones and will be able to assess which breed and size he prefers. He should have a much better idea of what is entailed in caring for horses, including the sort of saddle and bridle to buy. It is sometimes a good idea to keep the first horse at board (livery) for a while. Most riding schools welcome keen owners and encourage them to assist with the stable work, cleaning tack, etc. In this way, the rider will become more capable of caring for his horse at home, knowing when to get him re-shod or to call in a veterinarian, and understanding the feeding of horses in relation to their work and the tasks they perform.

Above: When mounting face the hindquarters and take the reins in the left hand close to the withers and the stirrup in the right.

Above: Place the left foot in the stirrup, keeping the toe low to avoid encouraging the horse to move off; the horse should remain still.

The horse can be mounted in a number of ways. The athletic rider can vault on—spring up to lie across the horse and then swing one leg over. Those too short to reach the stirrup (eg jockeys) can be legged up quite easily, but the most practical and safest way is to mount using the stirrup on the nearside (left). It is a tradition in the horse world to use the nearside as opposed to the offside (right) of the horse, as much as possible. Buckles and girths are done up that side, saddlery is put on from the nearside and the rider mounts from there.

Accidents do happen when mounting, especially if the rider becomes careless. The three important precautions to take are: choose a suitable site that is relatively peaceful and on firm ground; check the girths, as a saddle that slips around can frighten the horse and off-balance the rider; and if either horse or rider is inexperienced, get an assistant to hold the head, as the horse must stand still, both to avoid accidents and to establish discipline from the moment the rider gets on his back.

Below: When dismounting, remove the right foot from the stirrup to swing this leg over the saddle, taking the weight on the left leg. This rider has taken the left leg out of the stirrup to land on both.

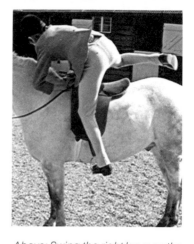

Above: With the right hand on the offside back of the saddle pull on both arms at the same time as putting weight onto the left foot.

Above: Swing the right leg over the back of the saddle and hind-quarters, lower into the saddle and put the feet into the stirrups.

The classical position of the rider on a horse is wholly practical and yet elegant. It places the rider over the horse's centre of gravity, which lies just behind the withers and roughly in line with the point of his shoulder.

To achieve the classical position

The rider must first take hold of the front of the saddle and pull himself forward until he is sitting in the deepest part, which should be just behind the arch of the saddle. Old-fashioned saddles with shallow seats will handicap the rider, and so will those that are very wide in the waist. Modern saddles, which should fit both the rider and the horse, are designed to help the rider to slide easily into the correct position.

Once the rider is sitting in the lowest part of the saddle he should make himself as tall and upright as possible. This is achieved by raising the upper body and by reaching down with the legs. Then, providing the waist and hips are not allowed to collapse backwards, his weight will come off the buttocks and on to the seat bones, the head will rise, the shoulders drop and the spine take up its natural line.

At the same time, the knee should be as low on the saddle as the rider's conformation permits, and the whole leg should lie close to the horse's side, with the toe higher than the heel. Once the rider has achieved this position it should be possible to draw an imaginary line from the lobe of his ear, through the point of his shoulder and his hip to the heel of the boot. He will then be in the basic position for all forms of riding on the flat, except racing.

If the imaginary line fails to touch the tip of the heel, the rider will be behind the balance and will probably have rounded his back and allowed his lower leg to swing forward. If the leg is behind the line, the rider is probably sitting on his fork. In other words, in the first instance he has transferred his weight back on to his buttocks,

and in the second he has gone forward off his seat bones and is balancing on his thighs. In neither position will his seat be stable and his weight related to that of the horse.

Even in the correct position the rider will not be able to maintain his seat once the horse is moving unless he is completely supple and relaxed. Any form of tension not only destroys his position but sets up a reciprocal stiffness in his horse, and this tends to make matters worse.

This particularly applies if he tries to grip with the knees or thighs. Contrary to what is sometimes believed this tends to weaken the rider's control by raising his seat out of the saddle. It defeats the whole object of the classical position, which depends on the united balance and harmony of horse and rider.

Thus, if the rider takes up the correct position and there is no tension in his body, he will be able to sink softly down into the horse's back on each stride (ie, as the hooves touch the ground). In this way the rider is carried up and gently forward by the horse's movement.

If, however, the rider is not seated over the horse's centre of gravity, the synchronization will be spoilt and the rider will have to maintain contact with the saddle by gripping and also to move his upper body to keep up with the horse's movement. Any dis-placement of the rider's weight that is out of harmony with the horse's natural balance is liable to set up mental and physical resistances, especially in the freedom of the horse's paces. Young animals in particular will be afraid of increas-ing their speed or lengthening their stride if they cannot rely on their burden to 'go with them'.

Provided his legs, and in particular the inner muscles of his thighs, are relaxed, the rider's knees will be deep on the saddle flap, and it is this depth that should help him to maintain his balance whatever the horse may do. At first, in his effort to lower the knee, the rider may find that his lower leg sticks out from the horse's side, but this tendency will correct itself once knee and leg are truly supple.

Then the rider will find that the inner side of his upper calf muscles automatically makes contact with the widest part of the horse's rib-cage, enabling him to give light unobtrusive aids. At the same time, because his upper body is upright and his shoulders are relaxed,the upper arms will hang down quite naturally until the point of his elbow lightly touches the hip bone. The rider has only to bring his forearm up until, when seen from the side, there is a straight line from his elbow down the rein to his horse's mouth for his arms to be in the right position as well. The hands should be held as though he were reading a book, with the fingers closed on the reins, the thumbs on top and the back of the wrists facing outward. If the rider maintains his balance without tension he is then able to use his hands and reins independently of the rest of his body.

To remain in the classical position, no matter what saddle or horse the rider may sit on, takes years of practice and is best learned by riding without stirrups while on the lunge. But it is essential that the instructor should be very experienced.

A rider in the established position will find that, by closing the angles of his hips, knees and ankles, he will be in the right place for jumping and galloping. For these activities, the imaginary line becomes shorter and runs directly from the rider's shoulder to his heel with the knee in front and the hips slightly behind. The rider is still in harmony with the horse's centre of gravity, with the body adjusted to comply with the horse's speed.

The principal object of the classical position is to allow the rider to be motionless in relation to the movement of the horse and for the two to work as one.

Below: This rider is in good position as a vertical line can be drawn from the lobe of his ear through shoulder and hip to his heel. The rider must be over the horse's centre of gravity.

THE WESTERN SEAT

The purpose of the Western (also known as the stock) seat is to permit a rider to assume a comfortable and relaxed position, so that he can spend many hours in the saddle, while still being able to control and guide his horse according to the demands of ranch and trail riding.

The high pommel and cantle of the Western saddle helps to achieve this by giving the rider greater security. The seat slopes backwards to the cantle so that the rider sits further back than is customary in the English style.

Western riders sit almost straight-legged, using longer stirrup leathers than in any other style of horsemanship. The leather must not be so long, however, that it is difficult to keep the heel below the toe. A deep seat enables the rider to brace himself in the saddle while roping and to effect the quick starts and stops needed in ranch work. The lower leg is vital to control and must be able to swing freely. Knees and thighs rest, but do not press, against the saddle.

Both reins are held in one hand, because cowboys need a free hand for holding a rope or to flap a

Below: Western riding with light rein contact for the extended walk.

Stetson at a stray calf. The reins normally pass through the fist from over the index or under the little finger with the thumb up. However, when the ends of split reins fall on the nearside, then one finger can be placed between the reins. The free hand and arm should hang down in a relaxed manner.

Western horses are taught neck-reining, a term that describes changing direction through rein pressure on the animal's neck. To turn left, for example, the rider lays the reins across the neck to the left, and the horse will respond to the combination of direct and indirect reining. The reins can be held in either hand.

A good stock seat position is best learned on a responsive but gentle horse. Picking up the rhythm at all gaits is essential, because any stiffness or awkwardness on the rider's part will 'show daylight' between him and the saddle. Unlike English-style equitation, Westerners do not post while trotting, so that a supple lower back and shock-absorbent legs are needed to sit down to a jog (the Western word for trot) as well as lope (the word for canter).

The aids should be imperceptible, and the weight of the rider must stay in the centre of the saddle.

The fundamental aim of the saddle seat position is to display a three- or five-gaited saddlebred or a Tennessee walking horse to the best advantage. A gaited horse or walker is characterized by a high degree of leg action that the rider wants to show off.

In the saddle seat position, the rider's legs are straighter than in the classic seat. Because gaited horses are trained to move forward with great energy, impulsion derived from leg pressure is less necessary in saddle seat equitation than in other disciplines. The rider is thus able to keep his legs ahead of the girth and slightly flared out at the knee, away from the horse.

To obtain the right position, the rider places himself comfortably in the saddle and finds his centre of gravity by sitting without irons and with slightly bent knees. The leathers can then be adjusted to the length needed to maintain the position. The iron is placed under the ball of the foot so that pressure on .the centre of the iron is equal across the entire width of the foot. The feet point straight ahead.

The rider holds his body erect. Arms are held higher and elbows stick out further than in the classic position. The purpose of this is to influence the horse's head carriage directly through rein pressure, so that the height of the hands depends on where the horse is carrying his head. Hands do not have to be held thumbs-up.

Some people believe that the saddle seat position is easier to learn than other styles because the rider's legs can be used to brace him in the saddle, and also because gaited horses are comfortable to ride. The novice rider starts at the walk, when a slight motion in the saddle is permissible. Particular attention must be paid to the animal's head carriage, which is set by a combination of curb and snaffle bit pressure, but no sawing action should be used. The saddle seat rider posts during the trot, and must learn to do so rapidly, in time to the gaited horse's animated leg action. The hips are kept under the body, so that there is no mechanical up-and-down motion nor a forward-and-backward swing. In the canter, 'the saddle should be polished' with the rider going with the horse, and this is easier to achieve on a Tennessee walking horse, which has a rocking chair canter.

Below: Using the saddle seat position to show off the horse's gait.

'Aids' is the well-chosen word for the methods used by riders to communicate with the horse. They both control and direct the horse in his work for man.

Throughout the ages the great horseman has sought to improve and refine his use of the aids until the communication between himself and his mount is such that they almost think as one. Even to come anywhere near this standard requires years of dedication and practice, but the aids used do not vary from those taught in any good riding school, and a high degree of proficiency is within the reach of most riders.

Natural and artificial aids
Aids are usually divided into two groups: the 'natural aids' are those given by means of the rider's body or voice; 'artificial aids' are those requiring some form of strap or gadget to achieve the right effect.

In the second group, only the whip and spurs have any part to play in the training of horses, but for practical purposes other things (such as martingales) may be advisable if horse or rider lacks experience.

The success or otherwise of using 'natural aids' is directly related to the ability of the rider to sit in the correct position in the saddle and to maintain the position under all circumstances: in other words, to be 'still' in relation to the movement of his horse. This is possible only if the rider is supple, relaxed and in command of all his muscular reactions. Involuntary or unco-ordinated movement on the part of the rider will either confuse the horse or, if repeated too frequently, cause him to 'stop listening'. This can easily turn a free, intelligent horse into a dull automaton. It is therefore up to the rider to ensure that he knows and uses the correct aids if he does not want his horse to become indifferent to them.

The legs
A horse's first line of defence is flight, and his immediate reaction

Above: The leg is being applied on the girth when it is used to generate forward movement.

to the pressure of the rider's legs is to move forward in an effort to escape. All riding is based on this reaction, and the horse's desire to move forward must never at any time be lost. Even in the most advanced dressage movements, impulsion must still be in a forward direction, although – in the piaffe, for example – he may be actually trotting on the spot. Once a horse learns that he can evade the rider's aids by going backwards or by conserving his energy, man is no longer master. Then the horse may develop such vices as rearing, napping or bucking, which make him a danger to himself and to his rider, who may be thrown off.

If the rider wishes his horse to be 'light' to the aids he should use only enough pressure with his legs (in particular with the inside of the upper calves) to remind the horse to go forward. This pressure should never be a steady squeeze or a heavy thump with the leg and heel, but a quick vibrant action with both legs on or just behind the girth. If the rider is sitting correctly, his legs will automatically touch this spot. No leg aid should be prolonged; if it is ineffective, it should be repeated once more

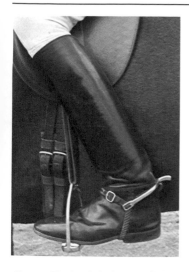

Above: The leg is being applied behind the girth when it is used to ask for lateral movement.

with greater firmness. Should the horse still not react it is wiser to use the whip, not as a punishment but to supplement the rider's legs. This is done by giving one short tap on the horse's ribs just behind the rider's leg. In other words, the rider asks the horse once or twice to go forward to the leg, and then, if necessary, demands it. It should be remembered that frequent use of the whip can nullify its effect as an aid, so it should never be used unless the rider's natural aids have failed and then only as a

refinement of that aid. The same can be said of the use of spurs, which must never be used as a punishment and are in any case not suitable for use on young horses or by inexperienced riders.

The hands
Once the horse moves forward it is the rider's task to control and direct the energy created. This he does through the reins to the horse's mouth. Once again, unless his seat is secure and his hands and arms supple he will be unable to use his hands independently of the rest of his body.

Unless the horse feels that he can go forward and touch the bit without experiencing pain, he will try to withdraw from it by ceasing to go forward or (in an effort to escape) will pull against it. If, however, the rider's contact with the horse's mouth is both light and steady and if the flexion in his wrists follows the natural movement of the horse's head and neck, the animal will relax his mouth and accept the bit as an aid to control and understanding.

It should never be forgotten how easy it is to damage the sensitive bars in the horse's mouth and that

Below: The snaffle rein is held correctly in this picture with the thumbs pointing upwards and the hands close to, but not resting on, the neck of the horse.

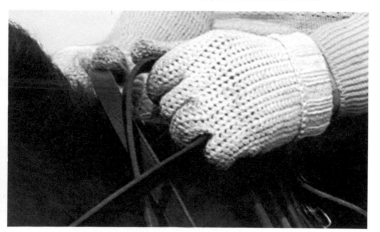

this contact is the rider's closest link with the horse's brain.

Except in rare circumstances the reins should be held in both hands with the snaffle reins lying between the fourth and fifth finger of each hand or, in the case of a double bridle, outside the little finger while the bit (curb) rein takes the place of the snaffle rein. The slack can then be taken up through the palm of the hand and allowed to hang over the top of the first finger, with the thumb resting lightly on top of it. The reins should be held short enough to enable the rider to keep a steady but light contact with the horse's mouth. His fingers should be closed because an open hand leaves nothing to give to the horse when following the natural

Below: The reins of a double bridle held in acceptable fashion with the bit rein around the outside of the little finger. The bit rein can also be held between the little and the fourth finger.

movement in his head and neck. The movement is most noticeable at the walk and trot, and the rider must always allow his hand to follow this without losing contact or allowing the rein to 'flap'. In this way, the rider's hands will be 'still' in relation to the horse's movement.

The reins should be used only to tell the horse either the speed or the direction at which he should proceed. At all other times they merely retain a steady but light contact. If, like the legs, they are used without thought—for instance, when the rider is talking to friends and not attending to his horse—the animal will soon stop listening and will no longer respond to the slightest change in the contact on the rein.

Thus it can be seen that the legs help to create forward impulsion and the hands decide how it should be used. This is done by varying the position and the degree to which these aids are used.

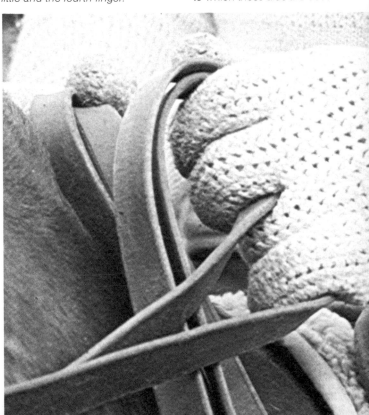

To turn a corner

The need to change the position of the leg and hand aids is partly to make a clear difference to the horse, who, having an amazing memory, will quickly associate the position with the required movements. The other reason is concerned with the way a horse actually moves. Once he knows that pressure of both the rider's legs is telling him to go forward, he will also move only one hind leg forward if he feels the increased pressure of that one of the rider's legs. On a circle the rider must apply his inside leg to ensure that the horse brings his inside hind leg not only well forward but also slightly under the weight of his body to maintain his balance while turning. Some of the impulsion created by this movement will then be carried diagonally forward towards the horse's outside shoulder. This impulsion is received and controlled by the outside rein: that is to say, the rider keeps a passive contact on this rein and, by closing his fingers, allows only sufficient of the impulsion to escape to maintain the required pace. At no time should this hand either lose contact or pull backwards. This is known as the passive outside rein controlling the pace while the rider's inside leg creates the impulsion.

At the same time the rider's outside leg should be very slightly behind the girth and ready to be applied if the horse tries to swing his quarters away from the pressure of the rider's inside leg. This is known as the outside leg holding or controlling the quarters. The role of the inside hand is to be very light and flexible and to ask for a slight bend in the direction of the circle.

When being ridden, a horse must be either going straight or turning, and these two basic positions and their appropriate aids apply from basic to advanced stages of training. The one thing that alters is the degree to which the aids are applied, as we shall see in later sections of the book.

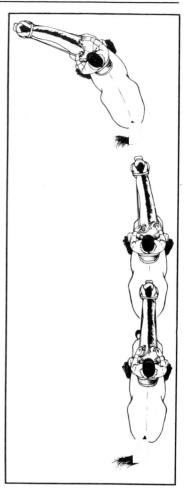

Above: This sequence of drawings illustrates the main points involved in turning a corner, a movement that needs careful control of the reins and use of the legs. The rider's head should be directed to look straight through the horse's ears. The outside leg is just behind the girth and stops the quarters from swinging out. The inside leg is on the girth; this is the most vital of all the aids when turning a corner. The inside rein asks for a slight bend, but the pressure should be less than on the outside rein. The outside rein controls the pace and should not be taken far from the neck.

USE OF AIDS

To trot

This is a two-time gait with the horse's legs moving in diagonal pairs (see Gaits of the Horse). The rider has two alternatives: 'to sit', when his seat does not leave the saddle, or 'to post' (to rise), when he sits in the saddle as one pair of the horse's diagonals comes to the ground and rises out of it as this same pair of diagonals leaves the ground. It is important that the horse is not made one sided by the rider always sitting for the same pair of diagonals. This is very easy to develop as every rider finds it more comfortable to sit to one particular diagonal pair. The rider must learn to change diagonals by sitting down in the saddle for an extra beat before starting to rise again. He should do this frequently when hacking, and when schooling should learn to sit to the outside diagonals (ie rise when the inside hind leg and outside foreleg come off the ground, and sit when this pair returns to the ground).

Below: The rider is rising from the saddle when one diagonal pair of legs is off the ground, and sitting for the other pair. Here he sits as the inside diagonals reach the ground.

To canter

The only other position the rider needs is that which tells his horse to change pace into the canter. At the canter (a three-time pace) the foreleg and hind leg on one side will be slightly in advance of the pair on the other side. Consequently it will be easier for the horse to describe a circle if the inside legs are leading. When the horse has learned to bring forward a hind leg in answer to a touch from the rider's leg, he can be asked to strike off on the required lead.

To induce him to strike off into the canter on the correct lead he should go into a corner slightly bent towards his leading foreleg. The rider's outside leg should be drawn back to tell him to move his outside hind leg forward. Then, according to the sequence of the canter (see Gaits of the Horse page 176), the inside hind leg and outside foreleg will now move forward together and he will finally lead with the inside foreleg. Thus the rider's outside leg tells the horse to bring forward that hind leg. It should not be applied too strongly or it would then be asking the hindquarters to move sideways, thus causing confusion

in the future when lateral work is taught. It is the rider's inside leg that asks for the forward impulsion, so it must be applied on the girth at the same time as the outside leg. Any reluctance or laziness to go into the canter should be remedied by stronger use of this inside (not outside) leg and if necessary a few

taps with the stick on the inside.

Once the horse has struck off into the canter, both the rider's legs return to the correct position at the girth to keep up the impulsion. Should the rider wish to change the canter lead, he first brings the horse back to the walk or trot and then reverses his canter aids. Eventually, when both he and his horse are well-balanced and have sufficient collection, the change can be made during the short period of suspension in the canter pace that comes immediately after the leading foreleg hits the ground. The horse will then change the sequence of his stride while in the air. This, known as the flying change, is quite natural to the horse when unmounted, but it is very difficult to teach a horse to change both hind and fore leading legs (they usually just change in front) before he has mastered the medium standard movements of dressage: that is, the horse is straight, performs lateral movements happily and is collected.

These demands are made of dressage horses only, as show-jumpers and polo ponies have to do flying changes and few are trained to medium dressage, but change automatically.
The three photographs at left illustrate the technique of striking off into the canter.

Top left: The rider is drawing his outside leg back, to brush along the horse, but not to dig into him, in order to indicate to him to bring his outside (off hind) forward and so strike off with the near foreleg leading. Centre left: In response to this the horse has brought his off hind leg much further forward than he did when trotting, although in this case he is offering some resistance by opening his mouth. Bottom left: The horse has struck off into the canter to lead with his near foreleg, and the rider is returning his right leg to its position close to the girth. The rider will keep using his inside leg to generate impulsion.

USE OF AIDS

The seat

So far this chapter has dealt only with the use of the hand and leg aids, but a correct and supple seat can play an immense part in training a horse. If the rider is sitting in the right position and is supple and relaxed, he has only to sink softly down in the saddle as the horse's hooves touch the ground to ensure that he and his mount rebound together. In this way, the rider will be in harmony with his horse and able to absorb the strong upward thrust of the horse's back through his own supple loins and thighs instead of being thrown off the saddle and falling stiffly back. The latter type of riding invariably causes the rider to start gripping in an effort to maintain his position and the horse to tense the muscles of his back in anticipation of the jar when the rider's seat returns to the saddle.

If, on the other hand, both are relaxed and the impulsion is being maintained, the deeper the rider sinks down with his horse the greater will be their joint recoil, and the horse's steps will become lighter and the stride more rounded and therefore shorter. This is the true way to obtain collection and has nothing to do with the false collection created when the horse's head and neck are positioned by the use of the reins or when he is merely slowed down to take shorter but less elevated strides. Neither method will produce the soft muscular roundness of outline with slightly lowered quarters that is the aim of collection. Few riders have the ability or the time to train their horses to achieve great collection, but once a rider has learned to appreciate the power that lies in the correct use of a supple seat he will find that all horses work much more freely and willingly for him and that he can use almost invisible hand and leg aids. This applies whether he requires a collected or an extended pace. The latter is directly dependent on the first because unless there is spring and height in the collected paces there will be insufficient time in the air for each set of legs to lengthen the stride. A rider who tries to obtain extension from a pace that lacks impulsion or by the use of rough leg aids will achieve nothing but greater speed and hurried strides, whereas true extension should be performed in the same rhythm as the other working, medium or collected paces.

The lateral aids

Once a horse is going freely forward and is 'straight', with the hind feet following in the track made by the fore feet, and once the rider is truly in control of the quarters, it is possible to start riding lateral movements. These are any movements where the quarters do not follow the same line as the horse's forehand and are often referred to as work on two tracks, encompassing such exercises as leg yielding, shoulder-in, renvers, travers and half pass. All are used to increase the horse's balance and obedience, the suppleness of the quarters and the joints, and the freedom of the shoulders.

In all cases, the horse must be going forward well. Only leg yielding can be performed in a working trot; all other lateral movements require a degree of collection whether carried out at a trot or at a canter. They do not, however, require the rider to use the legs in a different position from those he adopted when riding a turn or circle. By varying the degree of pressure of the leg just behind the girth, yet still maintaining impulsion by his seat and other leg at the girth, he will be able to move the quarters to left or right.

By riding straight forward while holding this position the horse will perform renvers (quarters out) or travers (quarters in). If the pressure on the outside leg (ie the one behind the girth) is increased, the horse will go forward and slightly to the side in half pass. If, on the other hand, the horse is ridden forward as though to start a circle until the forehand has left the track and the pressure of the inside leg — which is at the girth — is increased while the rider's opposite hand prevents him from continuing in the circle, the movement will be shoulder-in. If this movement is correctly executed it should be possible at any time to return to the circle by slightly relaxing the pressure of the leg at the girth and the opposite hand, thus allowing the horse to move forward again on one track into the circle.

None of these lateral movements should be attempted until the rider is confident that he can produce enough forward impulsion and can ride a true circle at all paces. Then he will need only to vary the use of his individual leg and hand aids to master all lateral work. As there is so little natural impulsion in

the walk, many advise against doing such exercises at this pace, because it can easily lose its regularity and sequence. It does, however, give the novice horse and/or rider a less hurried opportunity to understand the aids. Therefore as long as training at the walk is kept to a minimum and always followed immediately by some energetic movement straight forward, it can be beneficial. All lateral work can be done at the trot and eventually the canter.

Finally, whatever ambitions a rider may have, it cannot be stressed too strongly that if he and his horse are to reach their true potential every effort should be made to achieve the correct position in the saddle and to learn to use the aids effectively.

Below: The rider is performing the leg yield lateral movement.

Below: The shoulder-in, which is another lateral movement

JUMPING

Many people believe that jumping requires a different seat and aids from those used for riding on the flat. This is not the case. A jump is only a very elevated canter stride and the position when jumping is the same seat. All that has changed is that the rider has closed the angles at his hips, knees and ankles, enabling him to ride with shorter stirrup leathers, to lift his seat just clear of the saddle and to lean slightly forward over his horse's withers. The imaginary line that was discussed under the classical position would now go directly from the point of the rider's shoulder to his heel. In other words, although his weight remains over the horse's centre of gravity, his whole body is compressed like a spring. It is also important that the rider should not collapse at the waist or curve his back, which should at all times remain as flat as the natural line of his spine allows. The elbows may go rather further forward and the reins will be shorter, but there should still be a straight line through the rider's forearm and hand to the horse's mouth. As in the more upright position, all the rider's weight should be going down through his supple seat, thighs and knees.

In the jumping position it is not essential for the actual seat to touch the saddle. Some show-jumpers believe it is advantageous to bring the upper body into an upright position and to lower the seat into the saddle three or four strides in front of a fence. They feel that they can then use their seat to exert a greater influence over the horse. Show-jumping, however, is a very specialized sport and it is wiser for the less experienced rider to perfect a correct jumping position and to concentrate on maintaining that position while coming into a fence, going over it and landing. In this way he will be less likely to be left behind the horse's movement and to pull his horse in the mouth, and will also be in the correct position to go straight into the next stride after

landing. Once his position is truly established he will be able to influence the length of the horse's stride by using his legs and seat and by controlling with steady hands, which are independent of the rest of his body.

The position over the fence
Horses jump by dropping their weight on to their forelegs and bringing their hindquarters well under their centre of balance. As the forehand springs into the air the horse has time to tuck his forelegs under his chest before the hind legs hit the ground and propel his whole body over the fence. If the rider is sitting in a correct position and is supple and balanced, the less he moves or interferes with the horse the easier it will be for them both. As the horse's forehand rises, and the horse's hind legs come under the body, the withers will come closer to the rider's chest and the saddle will drop away from his seat. Relying on his balance and suppleness and, if necessary, gripping with his legs and particularly his knees against the saddle, the rider is ready to accept and go with the powerful forward thrust as the horse takes off. To make an efficient jump over the fence the horse has to round his back and to lower and stretch forward his neck and head. It is therefore necessary for the rider to give the horse sufficient length of rein to achieve this without actually losing contact. This he does by leaning forward, straightening his elbows and allowing his hands to go forward and down towards the horse's mouth. This must be done as the horse asks for the extra length of rein and not by throwing the rein forward and abandoning all contact, although this fault is better than causing the horse pain by getting left behind the movement and pulling on his mouth. This is serious because it soon causes a horse to lose confidence and to jump with a flat or hollow back. As the horse lands, the rider has only to rebend his

elbows to maintain contact and to be in the correct position for the next stride.

Position on landing

If the rider has maintained the forward position while over the jump he will be able to absorb the jar of the horse's forelegs touching the ground through his supple loins and thighs. Because his seat is still just clear of the saddle it will be easier for the horse to bring his hind legs well forward and under his body on landing. Then both horse and rider will be in the correct position to go straight forward into the next stride.

The rider's task

The rider's task is principally to ensure that the horse is going forward to the fence in a calm balanced manner with sufficient impulsion in each stride to release power at the right moment and propel both of them over the fence. An experienced rider can also help the horse by controlling the length of the stride so that they are able to take off from the correct spot relative to the height and width of the fence. But it should never be forgotten that once this place has been reached it is the horse who has to jump, and the rider can best assist by staying still in relation to the horse's movements. Riders who throw themselves forward by straightening the knees or who practise other acrobatic feats are usually only compensating for the inadequacy of their own position or lack of suppleness, and rarely help the horse. All too often such riders rely on their horse's speed and courage and then have to use rough methods to control and/or go with him over a fence.

Top right: The rider is allowing with her reins so that the horse can lower his head to look at the fence and prepare himself. Centre right: The rider has come forward too much, and she has lost contact with the reins. Bottom right: The rider is returning to her normal position a little late.

Basic Schooling

The aim of schooling is to teach a horse to understand, respect and gain confidence in his rider and to make him more supple, balanced and relaxed. Schooling will help the horse to use his ability to the full. He might have been able to jump high fences before training, but he will be able to do so for many more years and more successfully if he can work in a relaxed, efficient way, accepting help from his rider rather than relying on his agility to get out of difficulties.

ON THE FLAT

Impatient riders may try to by-pass the flat work in their haste to get on with the action; but a little patience pays dividends, extending a horse's working life and making the animal more pleasurable and successful to ride whether in racing, jumping, hunting, eventing or merely hacking around.

For the best results, good basic training is needed. This involves getting the horse to go forward rhythmically, straight and relaxed, with the hindquarters engaged and the rider maintaining a light elastic contact with the bit. To achieve this, the programme must be varied according to the horse's temperament, conformation and natural ability.

A suitable programme for an average young horse would start with 20 minutes' work in an arena, ridden or lunged, before being taken for a hack, and on the sixth day having a longer hack. This would not suit all temperaments or types, however. Weak, lazy horses need hacking to give them some excitement, including if possible plenty of hill work to build up the muscles. On the other hand, a neurotic horse would be more relaxed with longer periods of steady work in the arena. A nappy one must not be given an opportunity to misbehave: he should always go hacking with another horse, and should never be worked until bored in an arena. The trainer can experiment and must be alert and flexible so as to work out a really constructive programme that will develop the horse's strong points and overcome his weaknesses.

It is important to devise activities that are not too difficult for the stage of training and maturity that the horse has reached. Otherwise he may become crotchety, resisting if the work is beyond him. At the same time enough must be asked of the horse to keep him alert and attentive to the rider.

To go forward
This means first teaching the horse to respond to the rider's leg, making him want to go forward rather than slow up. This is best achieved by using the voice, and carrying a long schooling whip with which he can be tapped (not hit) just where the leg is applied.

To go on the bit
The horse must come to accept an elastic-like contact with the rider's hand, drawing toward the bit so that if the pressure is released he will try to find the contact again, rather than throw his head in the air with relief. He needs to have confidence in the gentleness of the rider's hands, so the rider must try to keep his hands steady but not stiff, maintaining a light contact with the mouth and not jerking or pulling. The bit should be a kind thick snaffle.

Engaging the hindquarters
This is necessary because they are the horse's source of impulsion and spring. The further they come under him the more power the horse will have (rather like compressing a spring). The rider asks the horse to place his

hindquarters further under him by using his legs and seat, while restraining him from going faster with a hand that resists but does not pull. It is very easy, however, for the impulsion created by these driving aids to escape if the horse is not accepting the bit. If the horse is above it (head too high), then he will tend to raise the head still higher when the legs are applied so that the effects of the driving action will disappear from the front.

The rider should aim at containing the driving action within the horse, ie, so that it goes 'through' from the horse's hindquarters to his body, then to the head and back along the reins to be felt by the rider's hands. If this is successful then the horse is under the rider's control, impulsion can be built up, and resistance, stiffness and loss of rhythm become much less likely to develop.

In most cases this is best achieved by getting the novice horse to go with a long low outline: ie, the top line of the back and neck is rounded and the head is stretched out and down. The horse might be a little on his forehand at first, but the rider should gradually ask more, using his legs and seat (never pulling on the reins). As the horse's hind legs come further underneath him, his body will be compressed and he will raise his head and neck. Taken very gradually, over months rather than weeks, the hollow outline can be avoided and the power of the horse should be controllable with the rider's driving aids being contained and not escaping.

Rhythm
As important in riding as in other sports. A horse that moves in rhythm is a balanced horse; with balance he is capable of jumping higher, galloping faster or performing dressage movements better. The horse must learn to walk (four hoofbeats), trot (two hoofbeats) and canter (three hoofbeats) rhythmically. Some horses have natural rhythm and

balance; others have to be taught. An excited horse will not learn easily, so the first aim must be to get him really calm and relaxed; conversely a lazy one will experience difficulty until he goes forward willingly, so he must be excited. After that it is up to the rider to remember the rhythm.

Straightness
This means the ability to turn in either direction without bias and to take contact with the bit evenly. All horses are born 'one-sided', finding it easier to turn one way than the other, and tending to take a stronger contact on one side of the bit than the other. They must therefore be 'suppled up', so that

crooked forward movement is avoided and the horse turns easily in both directions.

Suppling the stiff side is achieved by squeezing (not pulling) on the rein, and by applying pressure with the leg on the girth of the same side. The rein on the soft side should be held lightly. Eventually, though it may take a long time, the horse will relax his jaw on both sides and take an even contact.

Work to achieve these aims
Work can be done when riding across country, along paths and fields and up and down hills. It is usually easier to keep a horse wanting to go forward when out of doors, and changes of going and

different surroundings help his balance and teach him to look after himself. Going up hills makes the animal use his hind legs and develop his loin muscles; going down hills forces him to extend his shoulders and forelegs.

When riding, always be on the alert. Young horses may misbehave out of genuine fear or in an attempt to try to master their rider. A young horse must never be allowed to get his own way, but he must learn to relax at the same time. The rider should therefore be firm but never violent. If possible, always go out with another horse and always carry a long schooling whip. New demands will keep the horse absorbed.

Left: The horse is not going straight. He is hollowing towards his left side and the rein contact will be lighter.
Right and below: Schooling figures for arena or field. Work in an arena becomes boring for the horse if the rider is too unimaginative to keep his pupil's concentration. When schooling a horse keep his interest by varying your directions as shown here.

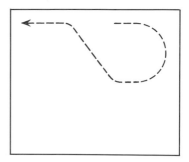

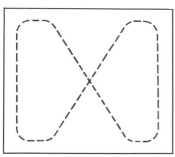

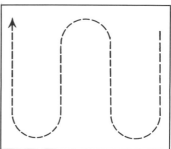

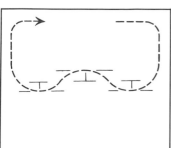

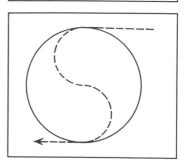

The movements

The walk can be easily ruined, because an untrained horse tends to tense up against the rider, losing the rhythm of the four hoofbeats. It is advisable to do no more than get the horse walking with a light contact on the bit until he is truly relaxed.

The trot

This requires a pronounced rhythm, and should be carried out at sufficient speed to make the strides both high and active. If too high, the trot may look pretty but the hock action will tend to be straight. If there is too much activity and speed, the trot will become rather flat and hurried.

At first the rider should post (rise) at the trot, only sitting for a few strides when the horse improves. If the horse does not lose his rhythm or go hollow in the back, and the rider is not thrown around, then he can sit for longer and longer periods. It is much

Below: Keeping a contact at the walk can cause resistance, and this horse is overbending.
Bottom: If a horse resists at the walk it is very easy for him to lose the rhythm of the four hoofbeats.

Below: A good trot. The diagonals are moving as pairs.
Centre: The outside diagonals are just coming off the ground.
Bottom: The outside diagonals have reached their highest level.

easier to control the horse from a sitting trot but if this is attempted too early the horse will become very stiff in the back.

The trot is usually the best pace at which to work a young horse, for the walk may make him tense and the canter is rarely sufficiently balanced. At the canter, it is more difficult to vary direction frequently because the leading leg has to be changed.

The canter

This should have a definite three-time hoofbeat and the danger is that it can easily turn into a four-time pace. It is important therefore that the horse must be kept going forward freely at all times.

Another danger is a disunited canter. The horse's inside foreleg

Below: The canter to the right in which the leading foreleg is about to come off the ground. This is followed by a short period of suspension when all the legs are off the ground. It is during this brief period of suspension that a flying change is made.

and hind leg should be in advance of the outside pair (leading with the inside legs). If he canters disunited (leading with the near foreleg and off hind leg or vice versa), the rider will feel uncomfortable and the horse will be unbalanced. He should be brought back to the trot immediately and the true canter re-established.

The most likely time for him to become disunited is if he strikes off into the canter on the wrong leg (with the outside legs leading, or counter canter). This will make it difficult to negotiate a corner and the horse will try to change. A young horse usually manages this only with the foreleg and thus becomes disunited. Always try to establish the correct lead from the start, by asking him to canter out of a circle. The animal should already be bending correctly, which will make it easier to strike off on the inside legs.

Turning a corner/circle

This may cause a young horse to want to change rhythm. This must not be allowed.

TURNING AND TRANSITIONS

Aim to keep the head slightly bent to the inside, with fore and hind legs moving on the same track, so that the hind legs do not swing outward or come inward. To achieve this the rider has to co-ordinate his hands and legs (see page 18). It is also important to prevent the horse from falling in to the inside of the circle (a very common fault), achieved by using the inside leg on the girth (further behind would push the quarter out). Avoid neck reining with the

Below and below right: As the horse starts to turn the rider twists his shoulders to keep them parallel with those of his horse. His outside leg can be seen resting against the horse, to be brought into play if the hindquarters swing out. The other vital aid is the outside rein, which is used to regulate the pace.

inside rein (a natural reaction) because, although this might stop the horse falling in, it will give him the wrong bend and make him stiff through his back.

Remember that in changing direction the bend in the neck should be altered to the inside.

Transitions from a slower to a faster pace
The aim is to keep the rein contact and the outline of the horse the same, so the rider must not lean forward and let the horse go faster, but sit upright and urge him forward with his seat and legs. The first step of the new pace should be high and upward, ie, the horse should not be pushed forward on to his forehand. From the walk to the trot both legs of the rider should close on the horse. From the trot to the canter the inside leg

is applied with a series of nudges on the girth. This is better than one hard one, which might startle the horse and lead to a change of outline. The outside leg is applied behind the girth: gently, if the horse tends to swing his quarters in: strongly if they come outward.

Transitions from a faster to a slower pace

Here, the aim is not to pull the horse backwards (the horse usually resists this by going above the bit), but simply not to allow him to go on at a faster pace. The rider sits deep in the saddle and applies the legs, pushing the horse to a resistant hand. From the canter to the trot, the rider sits deep in the saddle, while his hands resist the forward draw instead of following the movement of the canter. At the first step of the trot the horse must

be ridden forward to ensure the hindquarters are engaged. The same principle is followed when moving from the trot to the walk, and into a halt.

As the horse learns to relax during the transitions, he can be asked to go directly from the canter to the walk. Do not attempt this too early, however, or he will be too stiff in the back, will be unable to lower his hindquarters and will either go heavy on the hands, falling onto his shoulder, or resist by going above the bit and becoming hollow in the back. With this more demanding transition, extra encouragement from the rider's seat and legs is needed to get the horse to place his hindquarters well underneath. Make the transition progressive and not too abrupt as this produces resistances.

Training should bring out the best in the horse, by building up his confidence and agility through progressive work. In jumping, this means starting with poles and cavaletti so that the period between not jumping and jumping is so short that the horse is not aware of it. Try to ensure that the progress is never forced so that the horse can remain relaxed.

The cavaletti

The cavaletti consists of a pole 3m (10ft) in length that is bolted to a cross piece at either end so that it can be used at three heights simply by turning it over on to different sides. The longer the sections of the cross piece, the higher these heights will be, but the normal measurements are a 92cm (3ft) cross piece so the bar can be 25cm (10in), 38cm (15in) or 48cm (19in) high.

No training stable should be without cavaletti, which are easy to make, carry and adjust in height. When walking or trotting over them, the horse has to lift his legs high, which flexes the joints and teaches him to concentrate and to co-ordinate his limbs. By placing the cavaletti at equal distances apart, you develop the horse's rhythm; and putting them at a set distance in front of a fence ensures that the horse will take the right length of stride before take-off, without learning to accelerate and flatten.

To start with, use poles on the ground. As with all other obstacles, the horse should be shown them first. As long as the horse has time to look at them and sniff them, he has no excuse for stopping in fright. The rider, too, knows that he must ride firmly.

Start with one pole and then add more progressively (up to eight) at 1.2m (4ft) to 1.5m (5ft) intervals depending upon the size of the horse's stride. During all jumping training, it helps to have an assistant who can give advice, move poles and adjust distances.

As soon as the pupil has learned first to walk and then to trot over the poles calmly and without losing rhythm, then cavaletti can be introduced. They should be at the lowest height at first and the rider should aim at developing a springy rhythmical trot over them.

By introducing variations, the rider can teach his mount to lengthen or shorten his stride. When he is taking one stride at the trot between each cavaletti the distance between them can be extended to 3m (10ft) or more or less, according to the pupil. The distances should be shortened or lengthened by a few inches at a time, eventually introducing two short distances followed by two long ones (but never vice versa).

Below: Jumping a series of cavaletti at the canter. They have been placed 3m (10ft) apart, which is an easy distance for the average horse. Right: Three trotting poles 1.2-1.5m (4-5ft) apart have been placed in front of a hog's back made out of cavaletti. The poles make the horse flex his hocks.

The horse can then be taught to canter over cavaletti, popping straight in and out (2-3m/6-10ft apart). At the end of the line a parallel or hog's back could be placed (see picture) at either 3m (10ft) or 6m (20ft) from the last single cavaletti.

Another excellent exercise is to put the cavaletti in a circle with a diameter of about 20m (65ft) placing them either 1.5m (5ft) apart for trotting or 2.5-3m (8-10ft) for cantering. Alternatively, cavaletti can be scattered around, so that the horse can be trotted over them out of turns, on angles or in succession.

At all times the horse should trot or canter over the cavaletti with rhythm, balance and calmness. The rider must approach them as if there were nothing there. Tensing up, which spoils the horse's rhythm, can be overcome by breathing deeply or by shutting the eyes when on a straight line for the cavaletti.

The exercises may be carried out at the sitting or posting (rising) trot. More control and greater activity of the hindquarters is achieved at the sitting trot and it is therefore preferable unless the horse is too weak and stiff in the back to accept the rider's continual weight, or unless the rider has an insecure or heavy seat and finds it difficult to sit softly.

The distances mentioned are not standard. Horses and ponies have different lengths of stride, and sloping ground or heavy going (such as sand) also affect the length of stride. Trainers must use their common sense, and if in doubt experiment with the cavaletti at their lowest. If the distance appears wrong, change it immediately and do not persevere under the illusion that it ought to be right—there are no hard-and-fast measurements.

If the horse gets in a muddle because either the exercise was too difficult for him or a mistake had been made in the distance, go back to a simpler exercise.

A horse's jumping is difficult to improve but easy to spoil. Consequently it is vital to have an ideal to aim for, to keep a check on progress and, if the horse is failing to keep up the standard, to seek advice from an expert. Ideally, the horse should approach the fence in a balanced, calm manner, listening to the rider and with a rhythmic stride. He should then jump the fence with a bascule (lowering his head and neck and rounding his back so that it forms an arc), because this is the most efficient way of clearing a fence. On landing, he should re-establish the balanced, calm, rhythmical pace of the approach. Jumping in this way calls for relatively little mental and physical effort.

It is easy to hinder or destroy a horse's natural ability by getting him over-excited or allowing him to jump very flat or to refuse to jump. With few exceptions, these problems arise because rider and horse are advancing too fast, so that the horse fails to understand what is expected of him, finds jumping difficult and loses confidence. If this happens, the horse must immediately be taken back to the early stages and given some more work—some on the flat to get him obedient, and some over poles and cavaletti to help restore his rhythm and agility. The rate of progress will depend not only on the horse's natural ability but also on that of the rider. If they are both learning together then great patience and thoughtful training are needed.

Jumping without a rider
Most trainers believe that a horse should be without a rider when he is introduced to fences. It is wise to extend this stage if the rider has had little experience of teaching horses to jump. Jumping loose forces the horse to think for himself and relieves him of the anxiety of carrying a rider. It can take place on the lunge, or in an indoor or fenced school, or down a chute (enclosed lane) of fences. Riders lacking the latter facilities will have to make do with lungeing, and this is just as effective if the lunger works carefully.

In lungeing it is important, as always, to ask for only a little improvement at a time. Start with a pole on the ground before progressing to cavaletti and after a few days to a fence. Remember to show the horse each obstacle before asking him to go over it, and position the animal so that he arrives at the middle of the obstacle, and has two or three straight strides before having to take off. This

Above: On take-off the handler loosens contact on the lunge rein so the horse can lower his head. Red and white poles act as wings.

means that the lunger will have to be very active, moving quickly to get his pupil in the right place.

When the fence is introduced always place wings or sloping poles on either side to discourage the horse from running out, and ensure that the wings are low so that the lunge rein cannot get caught in them. When the horse is in the air, see that he has freedom to lower his head (the lunge rein must not be tight and the horse should not wear side reins). Finally, do not ask too much by starting jumping before he has warmed up with at least ten minutes at the trot and canter on the flat. Do not jump the horse for more than two or three consecutive circuits, but give him regular breaks of three or four circuits on the flat.

If the horse is to be jumped free in an enclosed school, start with a low fence, built with very large wings to prevent him from running out. Two or more assistants are needed to cover the school so that the pupil can be quietly but firmly encouraged (with the voice and cracking whips) to keep going around and

straight toward the fences.

Training a horse loose is invaluable as long as he is not excited through confused controls and does not discover, through incompetent or hesitant handling, that it is easier to go around the fence than over the top.

Jumping with the rider

When the horse has learned while free how to clear a fence in a relaxed manner, then the rider can take over. It is, however, an excellent idea to continue giving him occasional lessons free. The variety is good for him, and so is the opportunity to jump without relying on the rider.

The best way of introducing a fence is by extending the cavaletti lesson. For a 16hh horse, a 61cm (2ft) post and rails can be placed 6m (20ft) away from the last of three trotting poles or cavaletti at 1.5m (5ft) apart. In this way, as long as the rider helps the horse to keep up the rhythm and impulsion, he will arrive in a good place for take-off.

The rider is a vital aid in getting the horse to go calmly and confidently toward the fences. As he rides toward the fence he must reassure the animal that he is there to help, not to hinder. The reassurance comes largely from the rider's legs, which should feel as if they were enclosing the horse, and the tightening of the seat and legs on the approach encourages forward momentum. Some trainers like to give their horses a loose rein so that they learn to look after themselves and there is no risk of interference to the mouth from the rider. For competent riders, however, maintaining a light contact on the mouth (but not hooking or pulling) makes it easier to keep up the rhythm and to activate the hind legs. Choose one method or the other and stick to it. It is disturbing for the horse to expect a contact and lose it in the stride before take-off. Unfortunately, this is a common fault among riders, which makes it difficult for the animal to keep balanced, and can even ruin his confidence.

For the rider, the take-off can be tricky. At the trot it is difficult to judge the exact moment of take-off and the rider must be relaxed and have a good enough seat to be able to follow the horse's movements. If he anticipates the take-off he will unbalance his pupil; if he gets left behind, he may jab him in the mouth, which will make the horse fearful of using his head and neck. Unless the rider is confident of being able to follow the horse, it is best to jump on a loose rein and to put one hand on a neck strap.

Gridwork

Although most trainers prefer to introduce the early obstacles by setting them up after one or more cavaletti, opinions differ over the next stage of training. Some like to continue over single fences, others over grids (a line of fences with none, one or two strides between each). The danger of the grid is that unless distances are set correctly and measured frequently to ensure that fences have not been moved, they can create traps, perhaps causing a horse to crash into a fence. This could damage the horse's confidence, and it is best not to use grids unless there is an assistant to monitor their measurements.

A correctly measured grid builds up a horse's confidence, as the animal will always arrive at an easy take-off position. The rider can sit quietly without having to pull him back or push him forward, and this helps the animal to keep his balance and rhythm. Most important, however, the distances between the grid fences can be intentionally altered. A shorter distance teaches the horse to take shorter strides, to get close to the obstacles for take-off and to bascule to clear them. A greater distance encourages him to

Below: The two cavaletti help to engage the horse's hindquarters.

Below: The horse is in the middle of his non-jumping stride.

Below: The horse is about to take off, quite close to the fence.

extend his stride, to take off further back and to stretch himself in the air. The grids are thus excellent gymnastic exercises.

It is best always to start the grid line with one or two cavaletti or poles, as this helps to relax both horse and rider. The next fence can be 6m (20ft) away and the following 7.5m (23ft) apart for one stride or 10.5m (33ft) for two. The longer distance allows the horse to break into a canter. The fences can be between 61cm (2ft) and 1.07m (3ft 6in) high, and if a parallel is introduced the distance should be measured from the centre of the two poles.

Single fences

At first, single fences should be very low, between 61cm and 92cm (2-3ft), and it is best to jump them from the trot because the slower pace forces the horse to bascule in order to clear them. Here again, it is important to keep up a rhythm, so if the animal darts toward a fence, act as if not intending to jump it, and circle the horse quietly to one side. Re-establish the rhythm and try again. Remember not to haul the horse out at the last moment, as this might get him into the habit of running out or stopping.

Try to build a variety of fences to jump. At first, they should not be too alarming or painful to the horse if he knocks them down. Later, however, the fences should be made more imposing to encourage a horse to put in a better jump. A fairly solid fence will teach an animal that it is wiser to try to clear them.

A horse that can approach a 92 cm (3ft) fence with a good outline at a rhythmical, balanced trot and jump it with a good bascule can be considered to have completed his basic schooling both on the flat and over fences. He should now be ready to specialize.

Below: The horse is rounding himself well; the rider sits quietly.

Below: The horse is sizing up the upright poles one stride ahead.

Below: The rider is in a very good position as the horse leaps well.

Below: On landing note how the horse's pasterns are bent.

WHERE TO LEARN

For many centuries, Europeans have concentrated on the technique of riding, building up a large network of riding schools and developing a highly efficient system for producing trainers.

Riding schools and centres

Europeans are still the leaders in the world of equestrian education but other countries are following suit and today riding schools and centres are mushrooming all over the world. The facilities they offer range from a few ancient, work-worn ponies to the immaculate stables, indoor schools and extensive outdoor facilities of most up-to-date equestrian centres.

The United Kingdom

In the UK there are some 4,000 licensed riding schools, and it is illegal for anyone to accept payment for giving riding lessons on his own horse without first obtaining a license.

The classified pages of a telephone directory and advertisements in the local newspaper will yield the names of local riding schools; but such sources cannot tell an enquirer how good the schools may be. The British Horse Society and the Association of British Riding Schools both run approval schemes: any school approved by either body must conform to certain standards of stable management and instruction.

The BHS publishes an annual booklet, *Where to Ride,* which contains a list of riding schools in the UK. The riding schools are listed in three sections, 'approved' schools (in the BHS's opinion the best), 'recognized', or 'listed'.

The Association of British Riding Schools publishes its list of approved schools in a handbook, giving details of size, range of facilities and any specialities.

The UK's leading school is the National Equestrian Centre at Stoneleigh in Warwickshire. It was opened in 1967 with a view to making it a kind of university of the horse. A large number of different courses are run there and include refresher courses for qualified instructors to bring them up-to-date with new techniques. There are also training courses for selected young showjumpers and advanced courses taken by specialist instructors in dressage, jumping and combined training.

The United States

The American Horse Shows Association (AHSA) has set up a Riding Establishment Committee, which lays down standards to be met before a riding school can become a member of the AHSA.

In addition, state and regional Professional Horsemen's Associations have member-establishments, but membership does not necessarily indicate quality of horses or instruction.

The USA's most famous centre is at Gladstone, New Jersey, which is the home of the United States Equestrian Team's show-jumping and dressage squads. The three-day event squad opened its own Facility in Hamilton, Massachusetts.

The Potomac Horse Center in Maryland has been designed for men and women of any age with some riding experience. Potomac is well-known for dressage work.

The Bit o'Luck Stables are one of the newest large centres, specializing in dressage, cross-country and stadium jumping. They have three centres: at Alachua, Florida; Buck Hill Falls, Pa; and Middleburg, Va.

In October 1974, the Walnut stud farm at Lexington, Kentucky, became the Kentucky State Horse Park, the first state park devoted to horses and horsemastership.

Australia

Riding schools providing facilities from hack-hiring to instruction in advanced equitation exist in every state. There is no official control over riding schools, apart from local Board of Health regulations and zoning regulations. Surveys of riding schools and equestrian centres are published in *Australian Horse & Rider.*

Buying a Horse

Buying a horse is an absorbing, challenging and often hazardous business. The inexperienced can be taken in by wily sellers; even the experienced can misjudge a horse's quality. To make a successful purchase 'an eye for a horse' is needed—the ability to judge a horse's potential, to notice his good and weak points. The most important aspects to analyze are conformation and movement; soundness; suitability for proposed purpose; suitability for prospective rider; the personal preferences of the prospective owner; the future home; age; and value.

CONFORMATION

The first impression is important because it covers the overall proportions and appearance of the horse. All parts of the body should together form a harmonious whole. A head that looks too heavy for the neck to carry, for example, is not only ugly but weak and is likely to cause difficulty in establishing a good head carriage.

The head
The horse's character can be reasonably judged by studying the head. An eye that is bold, round and has a kind, generous expression is a generally reliable indication of good temperament. Any experienced buyer is suspicious of a horse that flashes his eyes nervously and looks backward frequently.

The position of the eyes is also important. Those placed wide apart usually belong to a horse or pony with a generous character. A fine, elegant head is usually a sign of a well-bred horse. More common features, however, usually indicate a more sensible temperament.

The neck
By its shape and length, the neck gives an indication of the natural head carriage, and only skilled riders can improve any defects. The neck should be in proportion. If it is too short, it makes a rider feel insecure, and the horse can balance himself only by holding it rather high; if too long, it is more difficult for the horse to support.

The most elegant and strongest shape for a neck is arched (convex top line). A straight line can normally be improved by corrective training, but a ewe neck (concave top line) is usually a permanent weakness.

The angle at which the neck joins the head is also important, as this affects respiration. If the depth from the poll to the jowl is particularly long then it will be difficult for the horse to flex without creasing the windpipe and restricting the flow of air along it.

The shoulders
The horse's movement and pulling strength can be judged by the shape of the shoulder. Thus a long, sloping shoulder, allowing more freedom of movement, is best for a riding horse. Long, sweeping strides rather than restricted ones can be taken. On the other hand, a straight shoulder provides more pulling power, and is favoured for carriage horses.

The back
This is the weight-bearing area, and indicates the strength and power of the horse. A short back makes a horse more stable and powerful, and gives him a greater weight-carrying capacity. An unduly short back, however, is not so supple, and can restrict the speed and action of the horse. Although a long back does make the horse more supple, it needs to be broad, muscular and supported by powerful loins to

Top: This horse has a hollow back, indicating possible weakness.

Above: The back is too straight; it should be slightly concave.

offset the weakness due to its length. Check this carefully.

The shape of the back should be slightly concave, though not too much, as a hollow back is weak (but bear in mind that a horse's back becomes hollower as he grows older). Shapes to be avoided are a sway-back (lower part of back wrenched) and a roach-back (convex top line), as both normally indicate a horse that is too weak to carry heavy loads.

The quarters
The horse's propulsive power, the spring to jump and the ability to gallop, is given by the quarters; the upper line should be rounded, not falling away or flat. Large, wide quarters indicate well-developed muscles, although, if they are too wide, the horse may tend to have a rolling action of the hind legs.

The breast
This should be relatively wide, so that the forelegs can operate freely and there is plenty of room in the chest for the lungs to expand fully.

The chest
If the chest is rounded and deep, it has 'heart room', and the capacity for heavy breathing; this is a good indication of the stamina of the horse. Depth, taken to be the distance from withers to belly, just behind the elbow, is considered one of the most reliable signs of a good horse.

The forelegs

These have to take the strain of the horse's weight, and absorb the concussion that results from galloping and jumping. Consequently they are the commonest seat of lameness in the horse, and prospective buyers should be very wary of buying any animal with weaknesses in this area. The legs should be almost straight as far as the pastern, which should slope obliquely toward the foot. The knees should be neither 'in' nor bowed and the feet should face straight forward. If they are turned inward or outward, such a twist is a weakness.

The knees

These should be clean, flat and well-defined. A horse that is 'over at the knee (convex outline) puts much less strain on his tendons than one that is 'back at the knee' (concave outline). The former rarely suffers from strained tendons.

The bone

The larger the circumference (assessed by measuring the leg

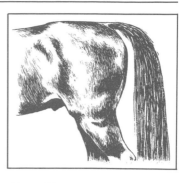

Above: The croup of this horse is too straight and the tail too high.

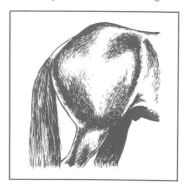

Above: The hindquarters shown here slope too steeply in shape.

Below left: Too narrow a breast.
Below right: Too shallow a chest.

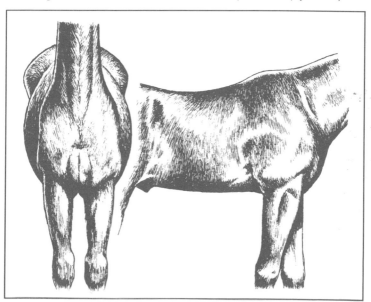

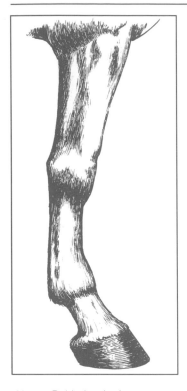

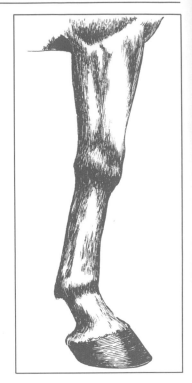

Above: Behind at the knee.

Above: Over at the knee.

below the knee), the greater the weight-carrying capacity of the horse. Also the flatter and more dense the bone, the greater the horse's chance of staying sound.

The fetlocks
These joints should be broad enough to provide a good area of articulation, and round joints must

be treated with suspicion; puffiness in the area of the fetlock joint is a sign of strain, and a warning that it cannot stand too much work. With a young horse, it suggests he has been brought on too quickly.

The pasterns
These should be neither too short

Below: A short and upright pastern.

Below: A long and sloping pastern.

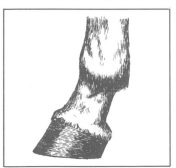

and upright, as this produces a bumpy ride; nor too long and sloping, as such pasterns are weak and place a greater strain on the tendons.

The tendons

Horses in demanding work (racing and eventing) are more liable to tendon trouble. The most reliable indications of weak tendons are:

1 Heat and soft swelling (puffiness) in the area of the tendon, which is usually evidence of a recent injury.
2 Hard swelling, in the form of either nodular lumps or overall filling, but without heat; this is evidence of a longstanding condition.
3 Heat and hard swelling.

In the case of the first, the horse may recover within a few days or it might be serious. It is better not to consider the immediate purchase of a horse in such a state but to ask to return when the heat and swelling have died down.

In the second instance, as long as the swelling is hard and cool, it is likely that the tissues have repaired. It is wise to find out, however, if the horse has been sound since the injury, and to get professional advice.

The third instance is the most serious, for it is likely to give continuous trouble.

The foot

As this is the base support for the horse it must be able to absorb jar, so a round and open-shaped hoof is best, providing a stronger and greater area to act as a shock absorber than one that is narrow, small or too upright. A large, flat foot, however, would be cumbersome. The feet should be symmetrical — matched in shape — so that the jar is shared evenly. The most important shock absorber, however, is the frog, which should be well-formed and in contact with the ground. A good blacksmith can do much to remedy defects of the frog.

Finally the material of the hoof should be strong and free from cracks, rings and any other signs of brittleness or crumbling.

The hind legs

These are a source of power and propulsion, most of which comes from the second thigh and the hock. Other points (joints, pasterns, etc) should be inspected for the same faults and good points as the front legs, paying good attention to the feet.

The second thigh

A broad, strong, muscular and relatively long second thigh is by far the most powerful.

The hock

This hardest-worked joint in the body is the source of much lameness, and weaknesses shown in it should, therefore, never be ignored. The shape should be wide from the front to the back; the quality should be

Below: A narrow foot; weak.

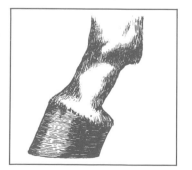

Below: A flat foot; cumbersome.

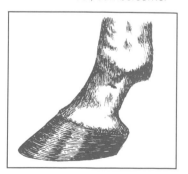

Above: A fine looking horse with good all round conformation.

high, with the bones neatly formed and well defined. Roundness and puffiness are warnings of possible

trouble developing in the hock.
The most common defects of the hock are:

1 Cow hocks, when the points of the hocks are turned in. As long as there are no other weak-

Below: A very straight hind leg.

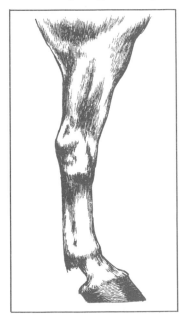

Below: A very bent hind leg.

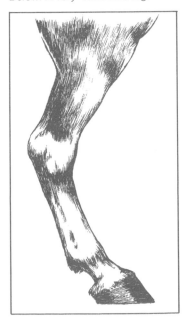

nesses of the hind legs, these are not a serious problem, although a horse with cow hocks does tend to take short, rolling steps.

2 Bowed hocks, which are the reverse of cow hocks. They usually result in the legs being set well apart and the toes turning inward. Bowed hocks usually lead to the hock twisting outward each time the leg is put to the ground, which places greater strain on this vital joint than can be easily borne.

3 Sickle hocks, in which the angle of the hocks is very acute and the hind legs are in the shape of a sickle. The more severe the angle, the greater the weakness.

4 Straight hocks, which are the opposite of sickle hocks, as the hock is structured so that there is a very large angle. Straight hocks result in rather stiff short strides and a lack of flexibility in the joints, which tends to put strain on the hind legs.

5 Curby hocks have a bony formation below the point of the hock, which can be seen when looked at from the side. Though an indication of weak hocks, this is not serious if there is no heat; and especially not if there are curbs on both hocks.

When considering the effect of any weakness of the limbs on the movement of the horse it is best to examine the shoes. Abnormal wear on the front or the side signifies that the movement is affected.

In the search for a horse it will be rare to find one without quite a number of the above defects, as the horse with perfect conformation does not exist. The main point to consider is how any defects will affect the work required of the horse. Few risks can be taken in the purchase of an eventer, but the buyer who wants a horse only for hacking need not worry too much about minor weaknesses. Remember that if a weakness does exist, but is supported by particularly sound and strong surrounding parts, there is much less cause for anxiety.

Below: Cow hocks; points turn in.   *Below: Bowed hocks; toes turn in.*

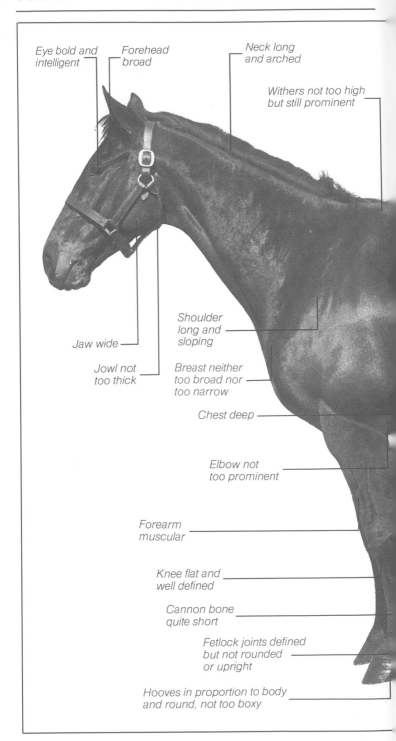

Eye bold and intelligent

Forehead broad

Neck long and arched

Withers not too high but still prominent

Shoulder long and sloping

Jaw wide

Jowl not too thick

Breast neither too broad nor too narrow

Chest deep

Elbow not too prominent

Forearm muscular

Knee flat and well defined

Cannon bone quite short

Fetlock joints defined but not rounded or upright

Hooves in proportion to body and round, not too boxy

GOOD FEATURES OF THE HORSE

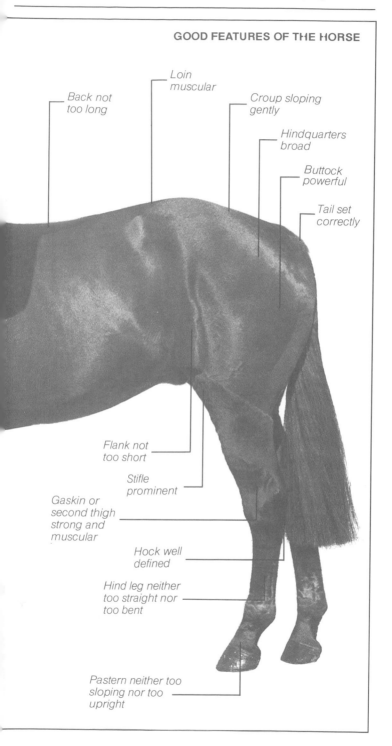

Back not
too long

Loin
muscular

Croup sloping
gently

Hindquarters
broad

Buttock
powerful

Tail set
correctly

Flank not
too short

Stifle
prominent

Gaskin or
second thigh
strong and
muscular

Hock well
defined

Hind leg neither
too straight nor
too bent

Pastern neither too
sloping nor too
upright

51

Movement

The horse should move with relatively straight strides. Swings and twists in action often place undue strain on one part of a limb. If the legs move close to one another, brushing can occur, although the effects of this can be prevented to some extent by the use of boots and bandages.

The forelegs should not swing inward and only a little outward (too much and the horse is said to 'dish'). The hind legs, too, should take relatively straight steps and (most important) should come well under the belly to provide driving power. The joints (especially the hocks) should articulate freely. They must not appear to restrict the action, producing stiffness.

The paces should be true—ie the walk four-time, the trot two-time and the canter three-time.

Horses used for different purposes need different styles of action. For those that pull carriages, a high knee action is acceptable; but if they are to gallop or to perform dressage, a freely moving shoulder and sweeping action are better. Generally, good jumpers do not have too long a stride and take athletic, springy steps, especially at the trot. For the racehorse the walk is the more important indication of value, because over-stepping by the hind foot of the fore foot on the opposite side and sweeping the ground is an indication of the ability to gallop.

Soundness

A magnificent animal to whom the proud new owner becomes nurse and payer of veterinary bills, rather than a rider, is of little use. Although the experienced purchaser can spot many signs of unsoundness, only a vet can make a reliable diagnosis. It is best, therefore, to arrange for a veterinary examination before paying for a horse. If the horse is expensive, it is worthwhile having X-rays taken of the feet, as these can expose serious problems.

When judging a horse for good movement, always look at the horse coming straight toward you so that any crooked movement becomes obvious. The bay shown above is moving straight and well. The grey shown below is not moving straight but twisting his foreleg, which puts great strain on his joints.

Suitability for proposed home
Buying a horse entails taking on an enormous responsibility. The amount of care and attention the animal needs, however, does vary from type to type. For example, if a purchaser has no stables and can only keep his animal at grass, then a hardy native breed (eg, Highland, Welsh Cob or Shetland) would be most suitable.

If the purchaser has a stable but is unable to provide constant supervision and daily exercise, then he can use the combined system of care when the horse is stabled by night in winter, and by day in summer, and turned out to grass for the other part of the 24 hours (in winter with a New Zealand rug). In this situation he

Below: A young rider well matched in size to a Welsh Mountain Pony. This native breed is sturdy and active – ideal as a child's pony. It can be kept at grass.

can think of buying a half-bred horse, which is more refined and usually has more performance ability than the native breed, but still has the toughness and good temperament to survive without constant attention.

If the purchaser wants an animal to carry him for long days of hunting or to do well in competitions, then he will need a horse with more class (closer to, if not wholly, Thoroughbred), and he must keep him fit. Such a horse needs constant attention in the stable and exercise every day; no purchaser should contemplate buying a high-grade refined animal unless he has the facilities and the time to cope with the enormous amount of work involved. There is, however, an option open to the ambitious rider with too little time to look after his horse, and that is to keep him at livery. As long as a reputable yard is chosen, then the professionals

can look after the animal and ride him when the owner is unable to do so.

Suitability for purpose

It is important to decide how much and what type of work will be demanded of the horse. Then the physical and temperamental assets needed to perform this work can be kept clearly in mind when examining possible animals.

Suitability for rider

It is vital that the horse is able to carry the weight of his owner, as an underhorsed rider not only looks unattractive but also puts great strain on the animal. The weight-carrying capacity of a horse is dependent on his height, depth, bone and chunkiness of body, although high-class animals— Thoroughbreds and Arabs— have denser bone and are able to carry comparatively more weight than a similarly shaped native breed.

It is important to make a fair assessment of the rider's ability, for it is no use buying a sensitive, athletic, class horse if the owner is not capable of controlling such a delicate creature. A novice rider needs a horse with a good temperament much more than one with ability. He must look for a co-operative partner, one that is not upset by confused aids and clumsy riding. There is little pleasure for the novice in riding a horse that can jump brilliantly but is highly excitable. There are exceptions, but inexperienced riders should not consider either horses with great ability (most have difficult temperaments) or Thoroughbreds (as riding these demands the greatest amount of horsemanship).

The character of the rider should be considered in relation to the type of horse to buy. The young, adventurous rider might enjoy and understand an excitable, forward-going horse. A more nervous, cautious rider will prefer a horse that needs urging on. This is one of the most important aspects of horse buying—choosing one that suits the buyer, and on whom he will produce good results. This is not necessarily the most brilliant horse that might be available.

Below: A handsome but unsuitable horse for this young rider. He will find it very difficult to control so large an animal.

Owning a horse is a pleasure, not a necessity, and the buyer who has personal preferences should, therefore, indulge them. 'If you like him, buy him' is, within reason, a good maxim.

Age

It is important to determine the age of the horse, and the prospective buyer's estimate can be confirmed by a veterinary examination. The main advantages of buying a younger horse are: he is less likely to have been spoiled or frightened; his potential has not been fully realized; and he can be trained in the buyer's

Below: Looking at a horse's teeth can give a fairly accurate idea of age. Up to the age of eight, the teeth undergo clear changes each year, after that age less so.

own way. A young horse's training, however, must be taken carefully, to avoid straining his immature limbs, although the pony, being smaller and tougher, can be brought on at a younger age than the horse. As he will have to be taught everything, he needs a patient, able rider. For the buyer who wants quick results, or who is not very capable, an older animal is advisable. This is especially the case with ponies. Wily horse-dealers break in ponies at two or three years, giving them little feed and much work. Prospective buyers are easily hoodwinked into believing the pony is older and has a good temperament. All too often, when the pony is taken to a new home and given more food and less work, his lack of training and youthful exuberance

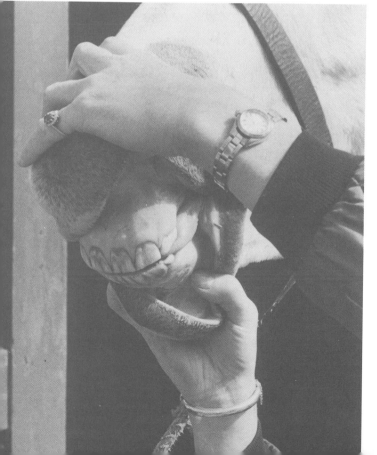

shine through, revealing him as a most unsuitable mount for a young and inexperienced rider.

Value

The price of a horse, unlike that of a car, is not necessarily an indication of quality; and certainly not of the horse's suitability for the rider. It is reasonable to ask: 'What is this horse worth to me?' It should be borne in mind, too, that upkeep is expensive. It is better for a buyer to pay a little more, if necessary, to acquire the horse he really wants; the costs of maintenance will then seem less of a burden.

Trying the horse

Start by inspecting the conformation of the animal, looking at him in and out of the stable and making note of his good points and weaknesses. Then feel for weaknesses by running the hands up the tendon, the cannon bone and over the joints, looking for splints (usually only on fore-legs), heat, puffiness. Lift up the feet, to ensure they are healthy and that the frog can touch the ground. Follow this close examination by asking to see the horse led away at the walk and then trotted back. Look out for weaknesses (particularly if the animal moves straight) and consider if the movement is suitable for the purpose intended.

Finally ask for the animal to be tacked up and watch the horse's reactions (fear, anger, etc), as this gives an insight into his character and past handling. Ask the owner or groom to ride the horse and show him on the flat and over fences. (If he is too young to be ridden, ask to see him lunged or running loose.)

If you are still interested, ask for a ride. It is a good idea to take the animal to a different place—such as an open field (to ensure that he is controllable), past the stables (to ensure he is not nappy, and unwilling to obey) and, if appropriate, into traffic. Taking into account his age and training, ask him to do as much as possible before making any decisions.

If the animal is to be a hunter, then most sellers will allow prospective purchasers to try him for a few hours with the local pack. This is an opportunity that will expose most major weaknesses that the horse may have.

The purchase
If the horse is suitable, then call in the vet to make his professional examination. He can advise whether in his opinion the animal is sound, and also whether the conformation is apt for his proposed use.

Some sellers will issue a warranty (a guarantee that they will take back the horse within a certain period if the animal fails to meet any of the specifications of the warranty, such as soundness, safeness in traffic, good manners out hunting, etc). If the buyer can obtain one of these it is to his advantage.

The other arrangement of benefit to purchasers is a trial. The horse is allowed to go to the prospective owner's home for a specified period to ensure that he is suitable. Although most sellers of ponies will allow a trial period, sellers of horses are less inclined to agree to such an arrangement.

Below: When buying, it is a good idea to see the horse on a long rein to check its movement.

Horse-dealers

Buying a horse from a dealer has certain advantages. He probably has a large stock of horses, giving the customer a wider selection. If none is liked, he usually has enough contacts in the horse-bartering world to know where a suitable animal may be found. Furthermore, he may be willing to take back a horse that proves unsuitable and find another.

The dealer, however, does not sell bargains. He has his own profit to make, and the price of the horse will reflect this. Some dealers, too, become over-anxious to make a sale and are possibly not above deceiving or at least over-persuading the naive customer. Finally, the dealer is a master of the art of making a horse look good, jump well, etc, so try to look beyond the first impressions that you may have.

Private sales

As private sellers are rarely profes-sionals, they tend to be more straightforward and less adept at covering up faults. To discover where a horse is being offered for sale privately, study newspapers and equestrian journals, which carry 'Horses for Sale' columns. For inexpensive horses, local papers are a good source. For competition horses, the specialist equestrian magazines should be scrutinized. Word-of-mouth and notices at tack shops and riding

Above: A pony sale in progress. The ponies for sale are paraded in the ring under the watchful eye of the auctioneer. Potential buyers look on and consult the catalogue.

schools are other fertile sources of information about impending sales.

Agencies

These are firms of specialists who, for a percentage of the final price, will relieve would-be buyers and sellers of the problems of searching for and finding out about a horse or locating a buyer.

Auctions

Auctions have long been the major market for Thoroughbreds, but have been less extensively used for the purchase and sale of other types of horse. With the growing interest in riding, how-ever, many more horses for private use are changing hands by means of auction sales than in the past.

At an auction sale there is usually a good number of horses to consider. The auctioneer carries out much of the routine work, which is convenient, and the price paid is the market value. The horse can rarely be given more than an on-the-spot examination, however, which makes it difficult to form a fair picture of ability and temperament. As the buyer's inspection is so limited, weak-nesses are more easily disguised and auctions have often been used as places to 'unload' bad horses. Also, bidding in itself needs experience. It is easy to be carried away by the atmosphere of the sale and to bid too highly and enthusiastically for the animal on offer in the ring.

When buying at an auction it is important to read the conditions of sale in the catalogue, particularly those covering the auctioneer's definition of a particular warranty, details of use of veterinary certificates and circumstances in which a horse is returnable. It is advisable to acquire the sale

Below: An auction held under cover. When bidding at auctions resist the temptation to offer too high a figure. Always try to examine the animals before the sale starts.

catalogue before the auction takes place so that it can be scrutinized in detail. It may be possible to inspect potential purchases at the sellers' homes.

On the day of the auction, carry out as extensive an examination as possible in the stable, have the horse led up and ask questions about it of all possible sources. If a horse is sold with a warranty, check *within the duration of the warranty* that the claims are true. If they are not, inform the auctioneers and arrange for the return of the horse. If a horse is bought with the right of re-examination by a veterinarian, arrange this for an early date. Remember that a veterinary certificate is only an expression of the opinion of a qualified practitioner; it is not a warranty with any legal weight.

An event horse. He has good depth implying he has stamina. The bone is sufficient to carry his body. His limbs are strong, and his feet good, which make it more likely for him to stand up to the rigours of eventing. He has plenty of 'class' about him (not too coarse or common) which should give him the ability to gallop.

A child's pony. This is a purebred Welsh—a breed which has enormous ability but sometimes their characters are a little too wilful to be ideal for children. The conformation of this one is good—stocky, compact and with a strong front. The outlook too looks genuine and kind, which is the most vital factor in a pony to be ridden by a child.

A polo pony. Although only 15hh he is wiry and tough enough to carry a big man at a gallop. He gives the appearance of being very athletic, able to turn quickly, accelerate rapidly into a gallop and stop within a few strides. He also has to be brave enough to allow his rider to 'ride off'—ie push opponents' ponies out of the way at a gallop.

A dressage horse. Like the show jumper powerful hindquarters are needed, but not necessarily to the extent of a 'jumping bump'. These well-rounded quarters are good enough and the front is very high class—a good sloping shoulder and a long well-crested neck. With such a shoulder the movement is likely to be good. The outlook certainly is, for the eye is generous and the ears broad, which implies that the horse has that asset important in dressage—a good temperament.

A Western horse. *Although not very big he appears tough and stocky enabling him to turn quickly, accelerate and carry a heavy weight. He is similar to the polo pony but stockier in order to be able to carry his rider for long hours on the ranch. The pinto marking was thought good camouflage in times of fighting, and is today rather fashionable.*

A hunter. *He has good bone enabling him to carry a good deal of weight for the long hours of hunting. He has an intelligent, bold outlook, implying he will take care of his rider across country. He has strong hindquarters to give him the power to jump and a good sloping shoulder to help him in galloping.*

A show-jumper. *The most important part is the hindquarters, as these generate the power to spring. This horse has a distinct 'jumping bump', that is, the croup is well pointed. He has also a good hind leg and in particular a well-developed second thigh. Although the forehand is not so important this horse's strong deep sloping shoulder will help in the thrust off the ground.*

A driving horse. *This horse is out of an Irish Draught mare. There is plenty of bone, and good feet to stand the hammering on the roads. The shoulder is much straighter than that of the dressage horse, which restricts the movement but gives more pulling power. The height of about 15.1hh is good as this gives it enough strength yet makes it more manoeuvrable than a bigger horse.*

Breeding Horses

Horse-breeding is one of the most rewarding occupations in the equestrian world. It provides the challenge of gathering information about prospective parents' pedigrees, performance records and conformation and using it to try to achieve the most complementary matings. Also it gives the great pleasure of seeing foals play, grow up and, with luck, do well in the activity for which they were bred.

PRINCIPLES OF SELECTION

Responsibilities of the breeder
Though common sense is the quality most essential to the aspiring horse-breeder, a responsible approach is also important. Mares and foals need attention; only horses used to the wild can be left to fend for themselves. Breeding is, moreover, a costly business; adequate shelter and food must be provided and veterinary assistance may sometimes be required.

Principles of selection
In view of the financial investment and the long period before results are achieved, considerable time and thought should be spent in preparation, particularly the careful selection of parents. Selection is one of the most intriguing aspects of breeding; in racing, where it reaches its most developed state, the question of basis of selection has attracted some of the best brains in the equestrian world.

Establishment of clear aims is the first stage. Two of the most important aims are to breed a sound animal and to establish the type of horse required.

To increase the chances of breeding a sound animal, parents with hereditary defects must be avoided. Defects include sickle and cow hocks, feet that turn in or out too much, very upright or sloping pasterns, a ewe neck, sway-back, parrot mouth, wind that is not clear (roarers or whistlers), eyes showing cataracts, legs with sidebones or spavins. The aim should be to use parents with good conformation, as a well-

proportioned horse is not only more pleasant to look at, but also more likely to stay sound. Horses that show weaknesses in conformation, however, need not be disregarded (as must those with hereditary defects) for breeding purposes; they can simply be mated with one whose shape offsets the problem. A mare with a short neck, for instance, can be put to a stallion with a long neck.

It is advisable to decide what work the offspring will be required to carry out (showing, jumping, farming, gymkhanas, etc), so that the breeder can build up a clear picture of the assets needed (ie, size, shape, temperament, specific ability).

After the objectives have been decided, selection can begin, and this is based on four sources of information which are carefully studied.

Appearance
Breeders can examine the appearance, movement and behaviour of prospective parents knowing that many of their features are likely to be passed on to their progeny. The mare, in addition, should have deep and broad hindquarters with wide hips, so that there is room for the foal go grow and be born; her genital organs and mammary glands should also be examined to make sure that they are normal.

Performance records
The performance records of mares and stallions in the show-ring, on the racecourse and

across country can be studied, as the progeny of successful parents is more likely to have ability than one from unsuccessful parents.

Pedigree
Appearance and performance records, though valuable, give an inadequate picture of genetic make-up; for instance, small mares can produce large stock. Examination of the conformation and performance of the grand-parents and great-grandparents, for example, helps to provide a more reliable basis of selection.

Produce
Studying the existing progeny of both mare and stallion is another valuable source of information on which to base selection. A stallion who 'stamps his stock' by trans-mitting definite characteristics is known as prepotent. Unfortunately, it takes time to prove a stallion's prepotency and the procedure for a mare is even slower. Most breeders have to rely on the previous three sources of information for their selection.

Choosing a stud
The other major consideration is to ensure that the mare will be well cared for if she is to be sent to a stud. Management of some studs is based on economy; feeding may be poor and mares with

foals, in particular, suffer from such treatment. Also, poor facilities are usually associated with low fertility in stallions. It is wise, therefore, to make a personal visit to the proposed stud, to find out as much as possible about it from other sources and, if the mare goes there, to make regular checks on her condition.

The stallion
Stallions (also known as studs or entires) vary in value from hundreds to millions of pounds or dollars, and the stud farms at which they stand range from ramshackle farm buildings to those where every possible equine luxury is provided.

A licence
In most countries, a licence must be obtained before a registered stallion can serve mares. The licence is issued after a veterinary examination has confirmed that the stallion will not pass on any hereditary disease, physical abnormality or infection.

Service fees
Fees are charged for mares visiting a stallion, and there are a number of ways this can be paid. For the services of the most valuable Thoroughbred stallions it is normal either to buy a share in

the stallion (up to 40 may be issued), or to buy a nomination that entitles the purchaser to send his mare for a service in that year. Nominations are usually bought at special auctions.

In general, however, a specified charge is made, either a straight fee demanded upon service or a fee payable only if a foal is born or the mare is certified in foal in the autumn. In the first case, the terms usually allow for a free return if the mare proves to be barren or the foal is born dead.

The stallions in the UK and USA are mainly privately owned, although some of those in England receive government subsidies. The UK scheme is operated through the Hunter Improvement Society, which receives a grant from the government to give selected stallions a premium. Consequently stallion owners can charge lower fees, and the services of the better horses are brought within the reach of most owners of mares.

The major contribution by governments towards breeding, however, is through their national studs. In the UK this is confined to

Below: The long-backed stallion at far left would be a bad partner for the mare on the right, but would be suitable for the shorter mare illustrated in the centre.

Thoroughbred horses, but over most of Europe the national studs house stallions ranging from ponies to riding horses to work horses.

The success of a stallion
This is measured by both his ability to breed good progeny and his fertility rate.

His chances of breeding good produce are increased if good mares are sent to him. In the early years when he is unproven these are best attracted by having good stud facilities where owners of mares know their property will be well treated, by advertising, and by the stallion possessing assets required in progeny (conformation, temperament, performance record, good pedigree).

Although a high fertility rate is inherent it can be improved by ensuring that the stallion is kept fit and contented.

Care of the stallion
In the past, stallions have often been treated as dangerous animals; it is now established, however, that the more normal their handling, the more reasonably they behave.

Stabling
The stallion can be stabled near other horses, because he enjoys their company, but it is inadvisable

to have mares in season too close for both their sakes.

Handling

This requires a combination of firmness and sympathy. The stallion must grow to trust and respect his handler, who should never show fear. In the case of ponies, Arabs and similar types, confident handling is not too difficult; but with larger and more excitable entires (eg Thoroughbreds), skill, courage and great understanding are required.

Below: A stallion being led by the stud groom to his mare. He is on a long lead line for the service. The stick is carried as stallions tend to bite, and is used to give him something to nibble. The halter is left on in case the bridle should break. He has no shoes behind to reduce the risk of damage.

Fitness

Some stallions serve more than 100 mares in a season, which is very strenuous work, so fitness is essential if high fertility is to be maintained.

The many tougher, less valuable stallions that live out and run with the mares require no special work to get fit. Most valuable stallions, however, are kept in. Some do have a small paddock or sand pit, with high, tough fencing, in which to run free; but they still need more work.

In the past, stallions were led out on regular walks lasting an hour or 90 minutes. This method of exercising is expensive and time-consuming, however, so lungeing or riding is more often used today. Both need skilful assistants; riding, in particular, calls for high-class horsemanship to ensure that these eruptive

creatures remain under control.

Feeding
During the stallion's rest time energy foods must be reduced, but as the working period approaches again they should be increased, together with proteins. Care must be taken not to give so much energy-producing food that the result is an unmanageable stallion. Skilful feeding is vital to health, well-being and fertility.

Worming, tooth filing and foot trimming
All these should be carried out at regular intervals. Any pain or indigestion will make a stallion reluctant to serve mares.

The mare
The heat, also called oestrum or season, lasts between five and seven days and normally occurs

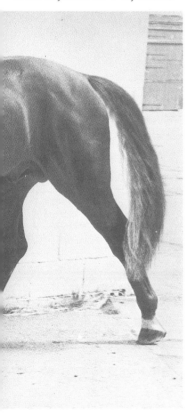

every three weeks, from spring to early autumn. Mares with foals come into season for two to four days beginning seven to ten days after foaling. It is only when the mare is in season that insemination can take place.

Puberty
This usually occurs at 15-24 months, though it sometimes does not take place until four years of age. It is thought inadvisable to serve mares before three years (except for well-grown two-year-olds).

Covering
In most cases mares are covered in the spring, so that the foal can benefit from the spring grass a year later. The fourth time a mare comes into season is more likely to produce successful results. Thoroughbreds intended for racing need to be covered earlier, however, so that their progeny is as mature as possible for the two- and three-year-old races. In the UK, February 15th is the official start of the Thoroughbred stud season.

A mare to be covered should be neither too fat nor too fit, but she will accept the stallion only when she is in season. She indicates that she is in season by seeking the company of other mares, raising her tail, passing urine frequently, with 'vulval winking' and protruding clitoris (a rod-like organ at the lip of the vulva), discharging mucus, and showing willingness to accept the stallion in the process known as 'teasing' or 'trying'.

Aids to getting a mare in season
The presence of a stallion, frequent teasing, the presence of other mares in season, and veterinary assistance such as hormone injections will all help get a mare in season.

Teasing or trying means taking the mare to the stallion and observing her reactions. If she is not in season, she may attack the stallion with teeth and hooves, so

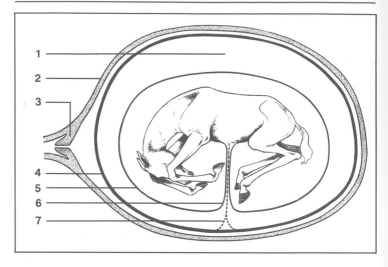

The embryo in the womb *(Above)*
1 *Allantoic fluid*
2 *Wall of the uterus*
3 *Cervix*
4 *Placenta*
5 *Amnion*
6 *Umbilical cord*
7 *Blood vessels running between the foetus and the placenta*

precautions are necessary. Such precautions include having a padded partition between the two horses, using a less valuable stallion called a teaser (if ready to be covered, the mare adopts a mating position, holding her tail to one side) and putting the mare in service hobbles and/or boots.

The service
This is usually carried out twice during the period a mare is in season. The fourth day is generally considered the best. It is advisable to have the mare swabbed before the service, which can be done only when she is in season, to ensure that she is clean.

A mare that has 'held' (is in foal) will refuse to accept a stallion when tried at her next scheduled heat periods (three weeks and six weeks). The cycle of sexual potency in a horse is, however, very irregular; up to eight weeks may pass between heats. Another

danger is that pregnant mares can have 'false heats'; if served during these, they may 'slip' (give premature birth to) their foals. Consequently, the mare must be examined regularly to ensure that she does not come back into season.

Pregnancy
The mare's failure to come back into season and rejecting the stallion is a sign of pregnancy, a veterinarian can examine the uterus. To confirm, use a blood test 50 days after mating and/or a urine test after 110 days.

Duration of pregnancy
Average duration is 11 months (336 days). A variation of ten days either way is normal, however; and with maiden mares the variation might be as much as two weeks either way.

The foetus
This develops within an outer membrane (bag of waters, or allantois) and an inner envelope (foal kell, or amnion), both of which contain fluid that insulates the foetus against blows or shocks. Nourishment of the foetus is achieved by a flow of blood between mare and foetus. The umbilical (navel) vein, enclosed in the navel cord, is the other

connection between the dam and the growing foetus.

Abortion (slipping the foal)
Kicks, blows, colic, chills, dusty poor food, over-exertion or infection can all cause abortion, and every precaution must be taken to prevent the mare from being subjected to these risks.

Work during pregnancy
The mare needs exercise right up to the time of foaling, but work should be graded; for the first five months, anything but exceptionally strenuous work is permissible. After this, the work should be gradually reduced; the mare should not be taken across rough terrain or over-exerted. During the last three and a half months, except for the very tough breeds, running free is the only advisable exercise.

Feeding
This will depend on the breed or type of mare. Ponies need only a few oats to supplement the grass in the winter time; Thoroughbreds will need much more supplementary food.

Points to remember
The foetus grows fastest in the second half of pregnancy, so the mare will need more food then. Too rich or dusty food can be harmful. Too little food will result in the mare's drawing on her own reserves, but too much bulk food will put pressure on the stomach.

During the last three weeks of pregnancy, reduce bulk food by half because there is less room in the mare's stomach.

Give her plenty of grass, and a bran mash once or twice a week, as there is a tendency for her to become constipated. Give supplements, available from most food manufacturers, and supplies of boiled linseed.

Below: A mare in foal. The pregnancy usually lasts about 336 days, during which time work loads should be gradually reduced but reasonable exercise maintained.

The foaling stall or box
This is needed for all but the tough breeds that foal outside, and should be at least 3·65m (12ft) square. It should be cleaned, disinfected and bedded down deeply; straw must be banked up the sides of the walls and door to help prevent draughts. The temperature should be kept at about 15°C (59°F). If possible, there should be a means of observing the mare without disturbing her.

The veterinarian
Especially in the case of Thoroughbred mares and/or if there are only inexperienced attendants available, a veterinarian may be needed during foaling. Consequently a veterinarian should be found who has stated willingness to attend and the telephone number must be placed in a prominent place.

Equipment
It is important that this should be readily available. Equipment includes two buckets that can be filled with warm water at the onset of labour; an old bucket for the afterbirth; cotton wool or gauze (gamgee); antiseptic powder or lotion for foal's navel stump; liquid paraffin, towels and soap.

Care of mare before foaling
Cut down the amount of hay, and correct, with a bran mash, any tendency for the droppings to harden. Gently handle the udder (mammary glands) to familiarize the mare (especially a maiden mare) with the sensation.

Indication of foaling
The udder starts to enlarge and is seen to be square when viewed from behind; this is known as 'bagging up' and can occur up to two weeks before foaling.

'Waxing up' takes place (drops of honey-like secretion form at the end of the teats), and although this usually happens in the last 24 hours before foaling it has been known to occur weeks before.

'Softening of the bones' occurs two weeks to a few hours before foaling, causing grooves to appear on either side of the root of the tail. The grooves are caused by the relaxation of muscles attached to the pelvis, to ease the passage of the foal. But it is possible for the mare to show none of these signs before foaling.

Signs of imminent foaling
The mare becomes restless, swishes her tail and starts to sweat as the time for foaling approaches. She may stale (pass urine) and get down and up again. The normal time for foaling to start is in the early hours of the morning.

Foaling down
The more natural the conditions and the less fussing done, the happier the mare will be, so stay out of the box as much as possible. Although most foalings are uneventful, it is advisable to have an experienced assistant available.

The normal contractions may not be seen. They start by being feeble and infrequent (one every five or ten minutes); but they should gradually become stronger and more frequent (one every half minute). Normally, within an hour from the start of contractions, the greyish water bag (the outer membrane of the foetus) appears between the lips of the vulva, then breaks to reveal the foal's forelegs wrapped in the yellowish membrane of the amnion.

When to seek veterinary advice
As long as the mare appears to be making reasonable progress, she is best left alone. However, if she is continually lying down and rising again without progress being made, and if the contractions become less frequent and/or more than an hour has passed since they started, then veterinary assistance should be sought in case serious difficulties arise.

Checking position of foal

When the foal appears under the tail, the position should be checked; the legs should be examined to see that knees, not hocks, are presenting. If the hocks are visible, then it is a breech presentation and a veterinarian or experienced helper is needed.

An experienced assistant can examine the mare to feel if the foal is in the correct 'diving' position (ie, both forefeet first and head straight and slightly behind). Before checking the position, the assistant should clean his hands and wrists with disinfectant and lubricate them with liquid paraffin. After this a skilled person can slide a hand into the birth passage and, if any problems are felt, make gentle manipulative adjustment. In the case of the slightest doubt, the veterinarian should be called.

A breech presentation is when the hind legs appear first. As the

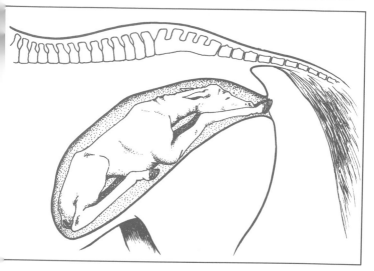

Above: A normal presentation.   Below: A breech presentation.

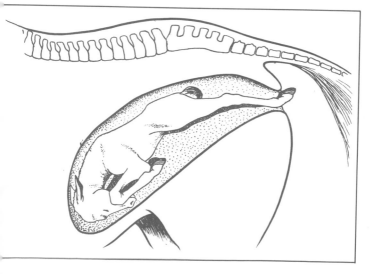

pelvis of the foal is broader than the skull, this angle of presentation makes foaling more difficult. The danger is that the umbilical cord is easily broken; if broken too soon, it can suffocate the foal. An experienced assistant may be able to pull the foal gently downwards and out (*never* straight) from the mare; but professional help is normally advisable.

Appearance of the foal

In a normal foaling, the chest and shoulders will follow after the forelegs appear, and the foal will then slide out, leaving only the last part of the hindquarters in the mare.

If the amnion does not burst after this process, the foal will suffocate; if necessary, the amnion should be broken by applying pressure between the foal's feet, while protecting his eyes from the straw.

At all times, care must be taken to disturb the mare as little as possible and not to try to hurry the process.

The umbilical cord should remain intact, because it supplies the foal with blood. Only when the foal starts to kick, freeing the hind legs, should the cord break. If this does not happen within a few minutes, the cord can be cut through with sterilized scissors at least four inches from the foal's belly. The stump should then be dressed with antiseptic powder or lotion. The cord should *not* be tied.

The amnion can be stripped from the foal and the mare encouraged to lick her offspring. This is the best means of stimulating the circulation and getting the foal dry. If the mare will not do it, the foal should be rubbed with a towel for about a quarter of an hour.

The afterbirth can then be tied up with twine so that it hangs at about the level of the hocks.

Care of the mare and foal

Healthy foals rise to their feet from 15 to 90 minutes after birth and start sucking milk. If the foal is weak, he may need assistance in standing up and finding his mother's udder. If the mare is a maiden or ticklish she may need to be held while the foal learns to suck. It is best to leave the mare alone until she has licked the foal; then she can be given a bran mash mixed with some linseed.

A stoppage
(no bowel movement)

This in the foal can be dangerous. Normally the foal should pass a small, hard piece of wax to free the anus within four to five hours of birth. If he does not and is standing with his tail up, then a mild enema, 1-2l (1¾-3½pt) of lukewarm soapy water, should be given. If there is no success after 18 hours, a veterinarian should be called.

If the mare does not cleanse
(expel the afterbirth)

If this has not occurred four hours after foaling, a veterinarian should be called.

Aftercare of mare and foal

For the first few days, the mare and foal (except for hardy breeds) are best kept indoors. Then they can be let out to graze, and, depending on the weather and the type of horse, can soon be left out all the time or brought in only at night.

Feeding

In the first few days after foaling the food is intended to have a laxative effect. Bran mashes are best. Supplementary food is needed throughout the summer, according to the type of mare and the degree of nourishment to be gained from grass. Thoroughbreds need 5-7kg (12-15lb) oats, boiled linseed and 7-9kg (15-20lb) hay. Most ponies need about 450g (1lb) oats and no hay as long as the grass is good. The important point, however, is to use common sense and if the mare and/or foal start going back, to give them more hard and bulk feed. Foals will soon begin to eat oats and Thoroughbreds can be given up to 450g (1lb) for each month of their life.

Inadequate milk production
This may occasionally be a problem. If the mare is not producing enough milk the foal will be seen repeatedly trying to suck. In this case the mare should be given more protein (clover, lucerne, bran and linseed) and if

this does not improve the milk supply, the veterinarian must be consulted.

Worming
This is extremely important; the mare should be wormed three weeks to a month before foaling, and then not again until after she

Below: A mare with her foal, just three weeks old. They should stay together for at least four months.

has been covered. The foal can be first wormed at eight weeks and then every month. The veterinarian will prescribe a dosage.

The feet
The foal's feet must be taken care of. They need regular trimming and picking out. If there are any deformities, corrections can often be made by the blacksmith; success is more likely when the bone is still relatively soft.

Weaning
The mare should not be separated from her progeny until the fourth month at the earliest. Thoroughbreds (except those that are weak and poorly formed) are usually weaned at five months, and other breeds at six months. If the mare is not in foal, weaning can be left until about eight months, as long as the mare is keeping in good condition.

Preparation for weaning
The mare's concentrates should be cut down in order to reduce her milk production. Mares out at grass are brought in seven to ten days before weaning, and the foals encouraged to learn to eat grain and hay. These should be given to them in containers separate from the mother's.

A stable or stall should be thickly bedded and any projections likely to injure the foal removed. For the last few days, the stable need not be mucked out; the mare's smell will remain in the box. The mare is led out quickly and taken far enough away to ensure that neither mare nor foal will hear the other's whinnies.

The foal is happier if left with other youngsters and he can be

turned out to grass with them after two or three days. The mare's milk dries off better if the udder is left alone. Milk her only if she is very full, as milking encourages further milk production.

Care of weaners
Supplementary feeding is necessary in the autumn after weaning because the grass is not so rich. A balance must be struck between over-feeding, which causes limb troubles, and under-feeding, which restricts growth. Good hay should be basic, plus up to 2·3kg (5lb) crushed oats (depending on breed), 450g (1lb) bran, mineral supplements, and small doses of cod liver oil and linseed.

Below: Young foals, only a few days old, enjoy each other's company and the freedom to roam in a well managed and spacious paddock.

Shelter
This is necessary during the winter. If stabled at night, however, the youngsters should be allowed to run free for exercise during the daylight hours.

Worming
After weaning this is essential, preferably following a veterinary prescription.

Growth
This is at its fastest during the first year, when 80 percent of the growth in height occurs. In the second year, the bone strengthens and the body deepens. A lack of care at these stages cannot be compensated for later.

Colts and fillies
These must be separated not later than 18 months.

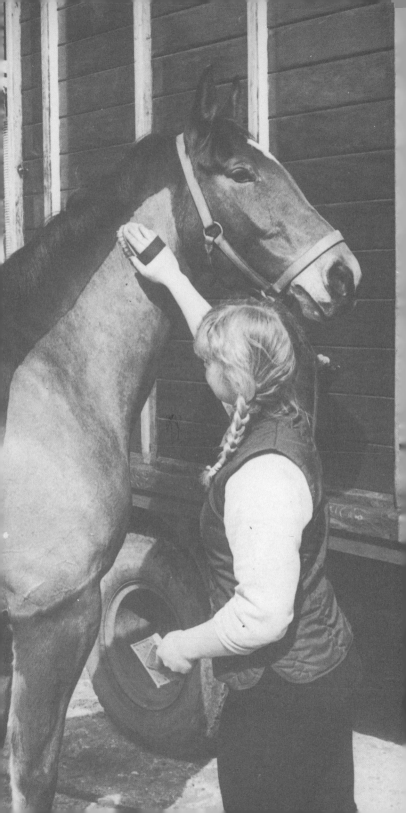

Care of the Horse

Horse riding has gained many new recruits. All over the world children and adults are taking up riding. This is a great development for the horse world, but only for the horses themselves if they are cared for with responsibility and knowledge. The following pages provide the vital information necessary for the horse's well-being, whether he is at grass, in the stable, ill or in the best of health. Everybody who looks after a horse or horses should be acquainted with this information.

AT GRASS

Supervision of horses at grass
Horses at grass have to be supervised. Otherwise they may damage themselves by kicking at one another or getting caught up in fences and gates. They can also very quickly lose condition through illness or bad weather. Daily checks are essential to ensure their well-being.

It is also important to handle livestock. Horses that are approached every day and patted, even when not being ridden, are unlikely to develop the infuriating habit of refusing to be caught.

The teeth of horses must be checked regularly. Rough edges on teeth make eating difficult and animals with this problem tend to lose condition. Feet, too, need constant attention. If the animal is not working, it is best to take the hind shoes off to reduce the risk of kicks damaging a field mate. Front shoes may be left on, but they must be removed regularly and hooves pared back. If the front shoes are taken off, the hooves must be trimmed at regular intervals and the feet examined for signs of cracking or crumbling. Many people recommend toe-clips as a good means of avoiding this.

The management of grassland
It is usually considered that about two to three acres per horse is sufficient. But it will be adequate only if the fields are looked after so that there is a good covering of grass. They should not be allowed to become weed-ridden, bare or poached so badly that there are potholes, ruts and mud. This means that looking after horses at grass also entails an elementary knowledge of grass management.

Horses are not good grazers. Unless it is a very large area, a field continuously grazed by them will become 'horse sick'. This means that the horses have cropped down the succulent grass and left the coarse and unpalatable remainder, so that the height of the grass is very uneven. In addition, their droppings further this unevenness by restricting growth where they fall and promoting tufts of weeds around them. Droppings are also a cause of red worm infestation of the field. It is important, therefore, to give the field a rest from horses (rotation) and to treat the grass.

Rotation
The best way of organizing rotation is to divide the land into small paddocks (if necessary, as small as half an acre) rather than have one large area. One area can then be grazed while the others are rested. A field should not be left full of horses until it is completely bare, for this makes it difficult for the grass to grow again. Ideally, when the horses are taken off they should be replaced by cattle, which are complementary grazers to them. Cattle like the long tufts, so they will level up the grass, and, as red worms do not survive when taken into their bodies, they also reduce

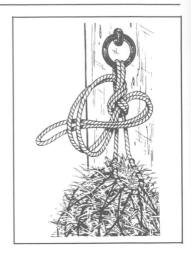

worm infestation. If there are no cattle to graze the land, the long tufts of grass should be cut down by hand or topped with a machine.

Harrowing and rolling

The second aspect of grass management is intelligent treatment of the grass. This entails chain harrowing and, if possible, rolling. Chain harrowing both aerates the soil by pulling out moss and matted growth and scatters harmful droppings. Many new horse owners will no doubt be horrified to read of the need to harrow horse-bound fields, envisaging expensive investments in a tractor and harrow. But frequently there is a friendly farmer nearby who will help by lending his machines, or harrows can be bought cheaply secondhand, and then towed by a truck, a Land Rover, or even a small car where the land is dry. Or, as happens in an increasing number of stables, a horse can be driven as well as ridden, and harrowing provides a very practical exercise for him. Finally, if all this fails, the fork and rake can be taken out for a few hours of good healthy work. If you find the effort tiring, remember that at most major studs the droppings are collected daily by hand.

The rolling of pastures is advisable, even if it is not as essential as harrowing. The treatment compacts the soil around the roots of the herbage after they have been pulled at and loosened by grazing horses. Heavy rains and frost disturb and loosen the topsoil, and compression by rolling will aid plant growth.

Fertilizing

Rotation, harrowing and rolling prevent pastures becoming horse sick and promote a good growth of grass. Growth can also be stimulated by fertilizing and the extra cost can be set against the fact that the additional grass will provide more feed. It is advisable to get a soil analysis made by an agricultural body, who can then suggest which materials are needed to counteract deficiencies. The most common recommendations are lime, basic slag (phosphatic fertilizer), potash salts (especially for sandy soils), nitrogen and simply manure, although the last should be applied only in the autumn and on fields destined for a hay crop in the spring, not for grazing.

Drainage

The final important improvement that can be made to keep grassland in good order is drainage. This is not so necessary for sandy and chalk land, which usually

drains adequately by itself, but in the case of clay it is often essential. Without drainage a clay soil is usually so boggy in winter that if the horses are turned out on it they will damage the grass by poaching it and probably get mud fever; in addition, there is unlikely to be much aeration in the subsoil, and this restricts plant growth. The digging of ditches around the field, and constant attention to keep them clear, helps drainage, but in the long run it is usually worth the expense of pipe drainage.

Feeding
Proper management of the grass will bring enormous gains in the feed value to grazing stock. However, no amount of care and attention will turn winter grass into nourishing foodstuff. Only in early spring to summer is the grass really rich, and by autumn it has lost nearly every beneficial quality except its value as bulk. This means that the majority of horses at grass will need supplementary feeding. No hard and fast rules can be made about this; the supervisor of the livestock must keep continual watch on their condition. As soon as an animal starts to lose weight, food must be provided — initially hay, and then, as condition deteriorates further, grain.

Native or wild breeds will need little, if any, supplementary feeding,

Above left to right: A round feed tin, a haynet tied up, a wooden feed box on a fence and a hay rack placed high up on a wall.

except in very bad weather. The more refined the breed, however, the greater the need to supplement the animal's natural diet. It should be added that even with supplementary feeding some horses, especially Thoroughbreds, suffer dreadfully from wintering out; so if stabling a horse is impossible it is more sensible to buy a hardy type that can withstand the rigours of winter.

There are times when the eating of grass must be restricted. In spring, when the grass is very rich, greedy horses often fill themselves to bursting point. This makes them too fat for their limbs, and can lead to the painful disease of laminitis. Consequently a horse that has such gluttonous habits should either be put on bare pasture, or be left free to eat the grass for only a few hours each day.

The other occasion when the eating of grass must be restricted is when the horse is being worked off grass. An animal will damage his limbs and his wind if asked to work hard when he is too fat. He will also need energy food, as grass only provides him with bulk.

The amount to feed at grass depends largely on common

sense, but the following points should be taken into account: the condition of the horse; the type of horse; the state of the grass; the season of the year; whether or not any work is being demanded of the grass-kept animal.

Utensils for feeding

Laying the hay out on the ground is very wasteful, as much of it will be trodden over and never eaten. It is better to use haynets, or even to buy one of the large hay racks built specifically for this purpose.

To feed grain, heavy round feeding bins are best, as light feeding bins get turned over easily.

Water

A constant supply of fresh, clean water is essential. A horse drinks about 35l (8gal) a day. An unpolluted stream is a suitable source of water, but stagnant ponds or pools must be fenced off. A large drinking trough is the easiest container; this can be in the form of an old enamel bath tub.

Shelter

The ideal field has some natural shelter, such as a stand of trees or a high hedge, which should provide the shade necessary in summer and the required protection from the wind and rain in winter. But such a natural shelter offers inadequate protection in snow and heavy rain, and actually attracts the flies that are such a menace to horses in the summertime. An artificial shelter can protect livestock against these hazards and, although horses will rarely use it except in extreme conditions, it is still worthwhile, especially as it can also provide a useful place for feeding.

An artificial field shelter need not be an elaborate structure provided it is sound enough to withstand winds. It should be at least the size of a loose box and be completely open on one side, but not into the sun; a narrow door might lead to quarrelling between animals, with the possibility of one horse being either permanently excluded or

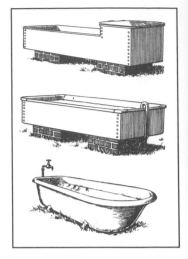

Top: A self-filling water tank.
Centre: A tank which has to be filled by turning on a tap, but this is underneath so the horse cannot be hurt by it.
Bottom: A horse could be injured by the tap or the lip around the bath.

trapped inside by the horses that are outside the shelter.

The safety of a field

A field is safe for horses only when there is a strong fence around its perimeter and when there are no objects in it that could cause damage, such as broken glass or pieces of wood etc.

The fence

It is worth spending money and time on a top-quality fence to avoid the inconvenience and danger of animals straying into the countryside and along the roads; poor fencing is one of the most common causes of horses being cut and damaged. Any fence must be high enough to stop horses jumping out—a minimum of about 1.13m (3ft 9in)—and strong enough to withstand being rubbed against, and it must have no pointed edges.

Of all forms of enclosure, stout post-and-rail (also called 'Man o'War') fencing, preferably three- or four-barred, is the best, both for appearance and for durability. A well-kept cut-and-laid hedge runs a close second. Hedges, unfortunately, are apt to develop weak spots and an inner rail may be necessary to prevent animals from pushing their way through. Stone walls are attractive and strong, but should be checked to see that they have not cracked and that the mortar is still intact. If they are drystone, make sure that none of the stones has shifted. Most people today, however, settle for wire, which is an excellent form of fencing if it has been properly erected. Plain, heavy-gauge, galvanized wire tightly strung between wooden creosoted posts is relatively cheap, and relatively safe provided that the lowest strand is no more than 30cm (1ft) from the ground and the wire does not sag. Electrified wire is becoming quite popular in the USA, and

Below: Two designs of field shelter with hay racks fixed inside.

appears to be surprisingly safe as the shock and jolt upon contact discourages the horse without injuring him.

There are types of fencing that can damage horses: these include barbed wire (especially if it is sagging), chicken mesh, spiked iron railings and sharp-pointed chestnut palings.

The gate
The gate needs to be easy for humans to open and close, but impossible for horses (it is surprising how ingenious a determined animal can be). Well-fitted five-bar gates are ideal; other means of closing and opening include slip rails secured by pins, or frame gates covered by galvanized steel mesh.

Poisonous plants and dangerous objects
The field should be checked, for glass bottles, cans, pieces of metal and plastic bags are often thrown

over the fence by passers-by, especially when a public footpath borders the field. Bottles and cans can lame a horse for life and it is not unknown for an animal to die after eating a plastic bag.

Any rabbit stops should be blocked up, as a horse can easily put his foot down one and this is especially dangerous to galloping animals.

Poisonous plants must be found and removed. Yew is particularly poisonous and dead clippings from this tree are fatal, as dead ragwort can be. Deadly nightshade

Below from top to bottom: Post and rail fence (safe but expensive), plain wire (safe if tight), broken barbed wire (very dangerous) and stone wall (safe if maintained).

is also toxic. Growing buttercups are poisonous, but the bitter taste of this plant makes most horses leave it alone. (In fact, once buttercups are cut and dried in hay, they completely lose their toxicity and are highly nutritious.) When ingested over a period of time, bracken may prove poisonous, although horses living in areas where bracken is common usually develop an immunity to it. Acorns, if eaten in large quantities, can have serious effects. Remember to check outside the fence as well as within, as horses will almost certainly stretch over to eat anything tempting that is within their reach.

Symptoms of poisoning
Purging, dryness of the mouth, dis-

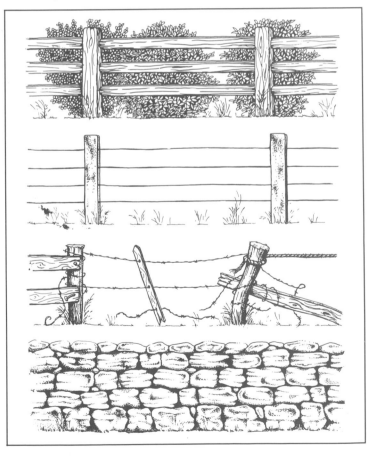

tension of the stomach, colic, excessive flow of saliva, giddiness, dilated pupils, convulsions or even paralysis are all indications of possible poisoning. If these develop in a horse at grass, it is important to act quickly. Take the victim into a stable and call the veterinarian.

Horses in work

Most horses, and all ponies, can be worked off grass. This has the advantage of avoiding the time-consuming routine of keeping them in a stable or stall. It also means that the animals need not be ridden every day, for they can exercise themselves. Care must be taken, however, to increase gradually the amount of work done off grass. Do not expect immediate fitness, and never demand fast work, or work of long duration, of grass-fed animals.

Grass provides bulk, but not energy food; so horses that are being hard ridden will need supplementary food (see pages 94-101). The most common subjects for working off grass are children's horses in the school vacations, and it is a good idea to start feeding them a few weeks before the vacation begins.

There are two other important points to bear in mind when grass-kept horses are in work. The first is that in cold weather the horse relies on the grease in his coat to keep him warm. In autumn and winter, therefore, grooming should be minimal, restricted merely to getting off the mud. The second point is that horses off grass, with shaggy coats, often sweat a great deal. If colds and colic are to be avoided, the animals must not be turned out until they are completely dry.

Keeping a horse at grass is less demanding than keeping him in the stable and, as long as he is cared for in a responsible fashion, can be very successful.

Right: Some common plants of the temperate regions known to poison horses (Latin names in brackets).

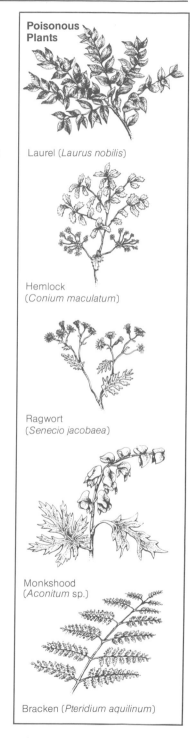

Poisonous Plants

Laurel (*Laurus nobilis*)

Hemlock (*Conium maculatum*)

Ragwort (*Senecio jacobaea*)

Monkshood (*Aconitum* sp.)

Bracken (*Pteridium aquilinum*)

IN THE STABLE

Reasons for stabling a horse

A horse may be stabled because the amount of work expected of him requires him to be in a fit condition, when he must carry no surplus flesh and his muscles must be firm, and this is impossible to achieve in a field. He has to become capable of arduous work without showing signs of distress, such as sweating or blowing, and to recover quickly from prolonged exertion. This hard condition takes time to achieve and is maintained only by giving enough of the correct type of food and the right amount of exercise. Such control is possible only in the stable.

Another reason for stabling a horse is that the animal may be too thin-skinned or constitutionally delicate to live out in all weathers. Some breeds have become so refined that they have lost the ability of native and wild breeds to bear bad weather. They cannot be left in the field throughout the winter months; if they were, they would lose condition even with special feeding supplements.

At board or livery

A delicate breed of horse, or one needed for hard work, has therefore to be stabled; but for owners who have neither the time nor the facilities to stable their horse there is an alternative—to keep him at board or livery. This is an expensive procedure. There are two ways of cutting costs, but both entail risks. The first is to choose a riding school and allow them to use the animal for others to ride. As long as he has a tolerant temperament and is used only by good riders, the system is satisfactory; but it is likely that at some time the horse will be treated carelessly, and possibly spoilt, by inexperienced or rough riders.

The second way of reducing costs is to choose a cut-rate stable. But, unless the lower price is due to the stable being run by a hardworking family business, the chances are that the costs are cut at the expense of your horse's food, exercise and general attention. It is important to carry out extensive research into possible stables, to determine whether the stable management is good and the exercising of the horses safe and efficient. Most countries have an officially organized system, run by the National Federation, under which riding schools and stables are inspected and graded. You should examine this list, and ask the opinion of people who already have horses in the proposed stables.

If you can pay the cost of boarding or livery, it is generally worthwhile to spend a little extra money to ensure that the horse's treatment will be first class. You will also be able to enjoy better hacking, schooling, and jumping facilities when you go to ride him.

When the stables have been chosen, the best way of ensuring that the horse is properly cared for is to take a keen interest in his condition and to make a habit of

discussing (without cross-examining) what work he has done in your absence. This interest will help to keep the stable managers on their toes and will also enable you to recognize quickly any deterioration in the well-being of the horse.

The stable

Any stable must conform to basic standards in size, strength, safety, ventilation, insulation and drainage. If you take over an existing stable, you should check to ensure that it conforms to the standards discussed below. If it is necessary to build, whether by converting such buildings as barns, garages, or cattle sheds, or by starting from scratch, then make certain that the plans conform to these same standards.

New stables can be either custom built, or prefabricated versions erected on a concrete base. The second is probably the

Above: A good example of well-made custom-built stables. This is probably the easiest and safest type of stable to build, providing secure comfort for the horse.

simpler and there are a number of manufacturers, producing stalls and stables of varying quality and size, who will provide plans and estimates. Most of these manufacturers will also erect the stables, but it may be cheaper to have it done by a local builder or even to do it yourself, if you have the necessary skill.

If you are building a new stable it will probably be necessary to get planning permission, and to adhere to local regulations about drainage and so on. These restrictions vary, usually according to how built-up the area is. It is worth taking the trouble to find out about local regulations. By keeping within them you will avoid later trouble with the authorities.

Below: A horse in a well-equipped stall (stable) with the window protected by a grill and a fitted manger in the corner for feed.

Above left and above: Horses in straight stalls with ball and rope.

The site should preferably be close to existing electricity and water supplies, as the stable will require both these services. It is usually best for the stable to face into the midday sun, and care should be taken that the prevailing wind will not blow straight through the doors. When designing the layout it is worth thinking about the view. Some owners prefer to give their horses something interesting to look at so that they do not become bored; others advocate a peaceful prospect for their animals so that they can rest. The preference depends largely on the work of the horse: those wanting quiet for their horses generally work them hard so that they are less likely to have the energy to get bored. Race-horses are a good example.

The stable, if built from scratch, should be laid out on 'time and motion' principles: in other words, there should be the least possible distance to cover to the vital sectors—feed room, storage facilities, tack room and manure pile.

The stables can be either straight stalls or loose boxes. In a straight stall the horse is always tied up by a rope or chain attached to his headcollar and running through a ring or hole in the manger to a light weight that rests on the floor of the stable. This gives him freedom of movement and enables him to lie down easily. The advantages of these stalls are that they can be relatively small, cleaning them out is much simpler because all the droppings are in one place, they are cheaper and easier to construct, and the horse is under better control. On the other hand, there is not much freedom for the occupants, and they tend to get bored staring at a wall all the time. In the UK and USA, where most owners are unusually sympathetic towards their horses' feelings, these stalls are rarely seen; but all over Europe, where labour for stablework is hard to come by, they are very common.

A box stall or loose box does enable the horses to move around, and must be more comfortable for the animal. But make sure that it is large enough to minimize the risk of a horse getting hurt or cast. This is when a horse rolls over, and his legs are stopped in mid-air by the wall. Lying on his back, he is unable to roll to the original position, and so is trapped until humans can hold his legs and pull him over.

The size will depend on the height of its occupant but the table below gives an idea of the size to choose for a box stall or loose box. Anyone choosing a small size for a small pony should remember that smaller ponies are often succeeded by bigger ones.

The doorway must be wide enough to allow the horse to pass through without bumping against the frame. It should therefore be at least 1.5m (4½ft) wide, preferably more, and not less than 2.25m (7½ft) high. Most stables have Dutch doors (in halves), although internal boxes in a barn may have only the lower half, or a grille instead of a solid top portion. Both halves should open up a full 180°, so that they can be fastened back against the stable wall. Bolts should be carefully fitted to prevent the horse from opening the door. The lower half should be fitted with a foot-operated kick-bolt at the bottom, or a conventional bolt, as well as a bolt at the top.

Special bolts can be bought that the horse cannot open, for many mischievous horses find out how to nuzzle open a bolt, and owners may find them either trotting around on investigatory tours or getting through dangerously large quantities of foodstuff in the feed room.

Ventilation should allow plenty of fresh air, but no draughts, as these at best make a horse uncomfortable, and at worst start chills and make the animal stiff. The wall should therefore be free of cracks and holes. Windows that open should be hinged at the base so that the wind blows in at the top. Whether or not to keep the top doors shut is a debatable point. It depends partly on whether the stable faces into the wind and partly on the work of the occupant. If a horse has to face cold winds and rain when being worked (hunting, for instance), then it is probably better not to coddle him too much in the stable, and to leave the top door open. If the animal leads a protected existence, however, and if a shiny coat would be of advantage, then he can be kept much warmer in the stable, although the atmosphere should never be allowed to become stuffy.

Insulation of stables is not essential, but is certainly of benefit. An extra layer on the wall will help to keep it cooler when the weather is hot, and warmer when the weather is cold. The second layer also makes it safer for a horse that tends to kick in the stable.

Roofs should be chosen for their insulation properties. Corrugated iron, although cheap, should not be used, because it is hot in summer and cold in winter. Wood or shingle covering is better.

STABLE CHART

Size of animal	Width	Length	Height
under 10hh	2¾m (9ft)	2¾m (9ft)	2½m (8½ft)
10-12hh	3m (10ft)	3m (10ft)	2¾m (9ft)
13-14.2hh	3¼m (11ft)	3¼m (11ft)	2¾m (9ft)
14.3-16.2hh	3½m (12ft)	3½m (12ft)	3m (10ft)
16.3-17hh	4m (13ft)	4m (13ft)	3m (10ft)
sick box foaling box	3½m (12ft)	4¾m (16ft)	3½-4¼m (12-14ft)

Above: A cast horse that cannot get his off foreleg and hind leg on the ground to give him the impetus to roll back. To help him up sit on his neck to keep his head on the ground, which will stop him struggling and hurting himself. Get an assistant to put a rope around both hind legs and a rope around both forelegs. Get off the neck and pull on the ropes to roll him back over so that he can get to his feet on his own.

Fittings are best kept to a minimum, to reduce the risk of a horse damaging himself on projections.

Windows provide the benefits of light and air, but can be dangerous if not protected. Horses can break them, and broken glass in the manger or on the floor may have serious consequences. It is therefore important to erect a grille on the inside of the window. If this is not possible, some wire mesh is usually sufficient protection.

Some horse-keepers do not have a manger fitted. Instead they give the feed in a container on the floor, which can be removed as soon as it has been cleared. This is satisfactory only if the feed tin is too heavy to be kicked or nuzzled over. For this reason plastic versions (except those specially designed not to be upset) should never be used. Iron feed tins or wooden feed boxes are thought to be the best types for general use.

The majority of stables, however, use fitted mangers, and these should be breast high. When choosing a type, ensure that it can be cleaned easily, and that it is broad enough to prevent the horse biting it and deep enough to stop the animal brushing the food out with his muzzle. Bars at the corners will also prevent food being brushed out.

Some stables use fitted hay racks, but there are disadvantages with these. The dust tends to fall into the eyes of the horse when he pulls out the hay, and also all over the person who fills it. It is better to use a haynet, which can be attached to a ring. The ring must be fitted firmly and at eye level. It is usual to fit a second similar ring to which the horse can be tied up.

It does save a great deal of time if automatically filling water bowls are fitted, but these should be sited away from the haynet and manger so that they do not become clogged with food. If using a bucket for water, a bucket container can be fitted breast high, but it is quite satisfactory to leave the bucket on the floor if it is heavy enough not to get upset.

All electric fittings must be out of the horse's reach. Switches should be of the outdoor variety and sited outside the stall or stable.

The floor of the stall or stable should be hard-wearing, non-porous and non-slip, and should slope slightly towards a drain or gully at one end. Concrete is the most popular form of flooring, but it must be dense and well compacted, and finished with a slip-proof treatment. A restless, stamping horse can quickly break up poor-quality concrete, so it is worth paying extra for the best. If a drain is fitted inside the box, it must be protected by a grille. Alternatively, a channel can carry urine through the wall to an outside drain.

The bedding, if abundant, reduces the risk of a horse injuring himself and encourages him to lie down. The bed should therefore be clean, dry, thickly laid and banked up around the walls. To keep it in good shape you will need a barrow, a shovel, one pitchfork with two prongs and one with four, a broom, a skep for droppings (this can be a plastic laundry basket) and a sheet of sackcloth or similar tough material for carrying straw.

Mucking out usually takes place first thing in the morning, when the manure and soiled bedding are separated from the clean bedding with the pitchfork, and taken away to the manure heap in the barrow. The dry bedding is forked into a heap so that the floor can be cleaned and aired before the bedding is relaid as a thinner day-bed. During the day, droppings should be picked up in the skep and removed to the manure heap. At night, the day-bed is tossed up and the new bedding laid on top, with the sides of the bed banked up higher against the walls. A good deep bed is not wasteful.

It saves both bedding and time to adopt a deep litter system, when only the droppings and wet patches are removed (but as frequently as possible) and small amounts of fresh bedding are added daily. The bed gradually builds up, and at some stage (every week, every month or every six months) must be removed in its entirety. The proud stable manager

rarely favours this method but it does save labour.

Handling the stabled horse in the stable is important towards establishing the same respectful but trusting relationship with the horse as when riding him. The animal must learn to be obedient and well-mannered, and not frightened or spoilt into becoming a kicker, biter or spiteful animal. From the first moment the handler must be gentle in action so as not to startle him, firm in requirements so as not to confuse him, and quick to reward obedience or to reprimand the animal (with the voice or a slap on the neck) if he misbehaves. At all times he should be approached from the head so that he can see what is happening. He should be talked to before any action is taken and during any handling. He will quickly learn the difference in tone between being soothed and being scolded.

Tying up is often thought unnecessary by trustful owners who may like to leave their horses free, but this is a mistake. A horse never becomes as obedient as a dog, and most of them will seize an opportunity to escape through the door. And when a horse is free in the stable, accidents happen so easily—pitchforks are stepped on, people kicked, and the like—so it is much fairer on the horse, and on everyone, to tie him up when mucking out, feeding, grooming and saddling up.

To tie the horse up, approach with the halter (headcollar) from the front, talk to him and pat his neck. Pass the free end of the rope around the neck. Put the noseband over the muzzle and the headpiece over the ears. A rope halter is then knotted on the near side of the horse, and a leather halter (headcollar) is buckled up. Lead him then to the ring on the wall and use a quick release knot.

Right: To muck out, the girl is using a four pronged pitchfork to lift the soiled bedding into the wheelbarrow. The broom and spade are left outside the stable.

Blanketing (rugging up) is necessary in all but the hottest weather for the horse kept in a stall or stable. To put it on, tie the horse up, take the blanket (rug) at the front and gently swing it over the horse to lie centrally along the back but high up on the neck. Buckle up the front and then slide back into position, but not so far that it drags on the shoulders.

If there is no surcingle attached to the blanket (rug), use a roller pad under a roller. Position this pad behind the withers and put the roller over it, ensuring that there are no twists in it at all. Buckle up the roller so that it is firm, but not squeezing the horse. Run the fingers between the roller and the rug to ensure that there are no lumps. Check that the rug is not too small, and is not pulling on the shoulders and withers, as this can make the animal sore.

In cold weather a clipped horse may need an additional blanket for warmth. This is put on first, again well forward, and slid back so that it nearly touches the

Below: This horse has been tied up correctly with the free end put through the loop so that the horse cannot pull the knot out.

root of the tail at the back. The blanket (rug) is then added, the roller done up and the free portion of the under blanket, at the front, folded back over the rug, to make it neat and stop it slipping back.

To take the blanket (rug) off, remove the roller and unfasten the front buckle. With the left hand grasp the part of the rug that is over the withers, and with the right hand the part over the back. Slide it off in the direction of the hair and fold it up four-square.

Stable routine

A timetable for a normal day in the stable is given here:

7am	Tie up horse and inspect for injury. Refill water bucket unless the stall has an automatic water fountain. Refill haynet. Muck out stable. Brush over horse without completely removing blanket (night rug). Pick out feet. Lay day-bed.
7.45am	Give the horse his first feed.
9.30am	Remove droppings. Remove rug. Saddle up and exercise the horse. On return refill water bucket.

Right: The correct sequence for rugging up. From top to bottom: The blanket is thrown gently over to fall on the neck, and slid back into place. The front buckle is done up, the roller is lifted on and, unless well padded, a pad is placed underneath. It is done up and any wrinkles smoothed out. In cold weather a clipped horse may need an extra blanket for warmth.

Noon	Tie up horse. Groom thoroughly. Put on blanket (day rug). Refill water bucket. Untie horse.
12.30pm	Give second feed. Refill haynet.
4.00pm	Tie up horse and pick out feet. Remove droppings and shake up bedding. Remove blanket (day rug), brush over and put on blanket (night rug). Refill water bucket. Untie horse.
5.00pm	Give third feed.
7.30pm	Remove droppings. Lay night-bed; refill water bucket and haynet.
8.00pm	Give final feed.
Last thing at night	Visit stable to ensure all is well.

The combined system

From this timetable, it can be seen that caring for a stable horse is a full-time occupation, unless the duties can be shared. If there is no one to help during the day, or it is difficult to exercise the horse regularly, it is better to turn him out into a field in the daytime, and stable him only at night. When the weather is very hot and the flies are troublesome during the day, the procedure can be reversed so that the horse is at grass during the night.

In the winter a stabled horse, especially if he is clipped, will find the fields very cold. The New Zealand rug has been specially designed to be worn by horses at grass. It is waterproof and has special straps to keep it in place even when the wearer rolls.

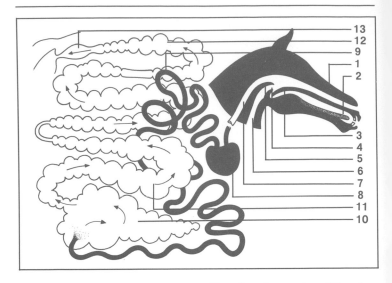

The digestive system *[Above]*
1. *Nasal passages*
2. *Tongue*
3. *Soft palate*
4. *Larynx*
5. *Pharynx*
6. *Windpipe*
7. *Gullet*
8. *Stomach*
9. *Small intestine*
10. *Large caecum*
11. *Large colon*
12. *Small colon*
13. *Rectum*

Horses have a very small stomach in relation to their size, and food passes through several digestive processes before waste matter is evacuated. The intestine narrows at various points, and bottle-necks can occur when food becomes impacted at these places; this leads to a build-up of doughy matter, the formation of gases, and ultimately an attack of colic.

It is essential, therefore, that horses should be fed small amounts several times a day and that their diet should contain plenty of fibrous foods to prevent impaction and fermentation. Grass, hay (dried grass) and, to a certain degree, bran (the outer husk of wheat grain) contain plenty of fibre. They also contain other nutrients, principally carbohydrates, some proteins, and minerals such as calcium, phosphorus and magnesium, as well as a number of essential trace elements. A horse that is required to do little work beyond gentle weekend hacking, and is living out with access to adequate grazing, needs no food other than grass in the summer and hay in the winter. Indeed, most native horses, with their powerful constitutions and extreme hardiness, fare better on a year-round diet composed entirely of grass or hay without any grain supplement.

But horses doing hard work, and refined breeds, require more proteins and carbohydrates than fields can provide. Proteins (nitrogenous substances) are needed to build and repair tissues (in particular, muscle tissue); and carbohydrates are needed for energy. Minerals and vitamins are also essential in small quantities; without them, health tends to decline, and such ailments as rickets develop in young stock.

Types of food
It is important to remember that concentrates rich in protein and carbohydrates are given in addition to grass and hay, never as substitutes. Bulk or roughage is essential to help the digestive process. Overfeeding of concen-

trates (especially protein) will upset the metabolism of the horse.

Hay

This is the staple diet of horses, however kept. The best hay for horses is seed hay, which contains a mixture of grasses especially sown for a hay crop (in other words, the hay comes from arable land where it is one of a rotation of crops). Clover hay, which is highly nutritious, should be mixed with another type of hay before feeding; on its own, it is too rich and heating for horses. Meadow hay comes from permanent grassland and may be good or bad, depending on its source. In many countries lucerne hay (alfalfa) is in common use. It is very rich in protein and a horse not used to eating it should be given only very small quantities at first.

Good-quality hay is greenish in colour, sweet smelling, free of dust, not too coarse, and between six and 18 months old. Yellow, blackish, damp or mouldy hay must be rejected, and every effort should be made to get good hay (the best if a horse is in fast work). Hay forms between one half and two thirds of the diet of a stabled horse and its quality will have a major effect on the animal's condition. During the winter months a horse may get through two tons of hay or more as part of its normal daily diet.

Bran

This is a by-product of the milling process of wheat. Although it is bulky and rich in proteins, bran contains relatively few energy-giving carbohydrates. The best bran is broad in flake, dry and not musty. It has a tendency to absorb moisture and become sour, so unless dry storage facilities are available it should be bought in small quantities.

Bran is used as a normal nutrient in daily feeds and in addition it can have a laxative effect if fed wet (dampened). Dampened bran mashes are usually given to mares in foal. In a normal feed it is

Above: Filling a haynet. The girl is taking small handfuls of hay from an opened bale, shaking them and pushing them into the net.

dampened, and is usually mixed with oats, in the ratio of three units of oats to one unit of bran.

Oats

This is the most effective energizing food for horses and must be used cautiously with spirited animals or children's mounts. Oats can be used whole but it is more usual to crush, roll or bruise them, so that the kernel is exposed to the digestive juices. This helps the process of digestion. Oats should not be crushed flat, which makes them lose their floury content, nor should they be kept for more than a few weeks after crushing, as they begin to lose their food value. The best oats are dry, without must, plump and short, more or less uniform in size and pale gold, light grey, dark chocolate brown or black in colour.

Barley

This is an excellent grain for improving condition. When used for this purpose, it should be boiled before being given to a horse. Raw barley should always be crushed and introduced to the diet very

95

gradually. It is not a good substitute for oats if the horse is used for very demanding or fast work.

Wheat
Except in very small quantities, this is not a suitable grain for horses. It should be crushed or boiled, then fed with other concentrates.

Corn (maize)
High in energy value but poor in proteins and minerals, it has good fattening effects but should not be fed in large quantities. It should never make up more than a quarter of the grain ration. As it is rather indigestible, it is best fed flaked.

Peas and beans
These are rich in protein and they should therefore be used sparingly, and only for a horse in hard work, one whose condition has deteriorated badly, or one that is wintering

Below: Samples of the main foods normally given to horses. 1 Barley 2 Oats 3 Compound food cubes 4 Carrots 5 Cod liver oil 6 Bran 7 Chaff 8 Sugar beet pulp cubes.

out at grass. Peas and beans should be split or crushed with a hammer before being mixed with the feed.

Sugar beet
Usually available dried and pulped, this must be soaked in water overnight before being mixed with the feed. If fed dry it would swell in the stomach, and could cause colic. It is a good conditioner.

Horse cubes
Known in the USA as pellets, these contain most of the required nutrients in well-balanced proportions. According to the market for grain, they are made up of varying quantities of oats, bran, maize, barley, locust bean, linseed cake, groundnut meal, grass meal, molasses, vitamins and minerals. They have great advantages as a foodstuff. They are convenient to store, and as they provide a balanced diet they can be used on their own, making it unnecessary to mix the feed. Because they create less energy, they are an especially beneficial substitute for oats when feeding spirited horses

and children's mounts. Their only drawback is that they are relatively expensive.

Chaff
This is chopped hay or oat straw. About 450g (1lb) of chaff should be added to all feeds, as it ensures proper chewing of concentrates and acts as an abrasive on teeth. The chaff sold by feed merchants tends to be of very poor quality and is therefore of little use. The only sure way of getting good chaff is to use a chaff cutter; these can be bought secondhand, or perhaps a neighbour will lend one at regular intervals.

If neither of these alternatives is possible, chaff may be left out of the diet; although advisable, it is not essential. Bran and horse cubes both to some extent stop the horse bolting its food.

Root vegetables
These help to provide variety and a different taste for horses that are stabled. Roots are of special value to poor feeders and to horses in bad condition. Carrots are probably the best, but turnips,

mangels, swedes and parsnips are thoroughly appreciated by most horses. Roots should be sliced into finger-shaped pieces and mixed with the regular food.

Molasses
This may be sprinkled on a feed, to encourage a finicky eater or to promote a shiny coat. It should never be used to disguise mouldy, dusty or poor-quality hay. Hay in bad condition will not become more nutritious as a result of being made more palatable, and it may even be harmful.

Cod liver oil
This helps to build up condition and improve the horse's coat. As it has an unpleasant taste, manufacturers make it more attractive to shy feeders by mixing it with more tasty materials. It is then sold under a brand name as either cake or in a liquid form.

Mineral salt licks
There are a number of mineral salt licks available, which can be fixed into special containers and attached to the wall, or simply left in the manger. Some horse-keepers, however, prefer to use lumps of rock salt rather than these prepared licks.

Linseed
This is rich in oil, which makes it an excellent means of improving condition and giving gloss to a coat. It must be well cooked to destroy the poisonous enzyme that is present in raw linseed. The linseed can be made into a jelly or tea, according to the amount of water used. To make jelly, soak the linseed in water for 24 hours, then add more water and bring to the boil. After being allowed to cool, the jelly is tipped out and mixed with the feed. Linseed tea is prepared in the same way as jelly but more water is added; the resulting liquid can be used to make linseed mash. Linseed can also be bought as cubes and fed directly, which relieves the feeder of this preparation process.

FEEDING AND WATERING

A bran mash
Usually fed the night before a rest day, or after a great exertion, such as a day's hunting, it is an excellent laxative. To make it, pour boiling water over half a bucket of bran, stir it well, cover with a sack, and leave it to steam until it is cool enough to be eaten. The mash should be 'crumbled dry', neither stiff nor watery. About a quarter of an ounce (7g) of salt may be added to half a bucket of bran.

Basics of good feeding in the stable
1 Feed little and often. Times of feed will vary according to stable routine, but an acceptable time-table would be feeds at 7.45 am, 12.30 pm, 5.00 pm and 8.00 pm.
2 Feed plenty of bulk food (hay or grass). Using a haynet prevents hay from being wasted, but it should be tied securely and high enough to prevent the horse getting his feet tangled in it. A haynet should be given about three times a day, and the total quantity divided unevenly, with the smallest amount in the morning and the largest amount in the evening.
3 The amount of the feed should be adjusted according to the work being done by the horse and the size and temperament of the animal. A horse that becomes excitable and difficult to manage should have his oat ration decreased; cubes should be given instead.
4 Any change in types of food or times of feed should be gradual and spread over several days.
5 Avoid using musty, dusty food-stuffs and always dampen (but do not soak) the feed.
6 Do not work a horse hard immediately after feeding, or when the stomach is full of grass. Quiet work is possible

FEEDING CHART

TYPE OF HORSE	7.45am	12.30pm
Hunter, working or event horse more than 16hh	2lb oats, 1lb bran plus chaff, 2lb hay	3lb oats, 1lb bran plus chaff, 5lb hay
Hunter, working or event horse less than 16hh	2lb oats, 1lb bran plus chaff, 2lb hay	3lb oats, 1lb bran plus chaff, 4lb hay
14.2hh pony, working, hunting or eventing (turned out for a few hours)	2lb cubes, 1lb bran, chaff, 2lb hay	turned out
Show-jumper over 16hh	2lb oats, 1lb bran, chaff, 2lb hay	2lb oats, 1lb cubes, 1lb bran, chaff, 5lb hay
Riding horse of about 15hh (turned out by night in summer, or for a few hours during the day)	1lb oats, 2lb cubes, 1lb bran, 2lb hay	1lb oats, 2lb cubes, 1lb flaked maize, 1lb bran, chaff 3lb hay
Child's pony of about 13.2hh being worked daily (but turned out for a few hours)	1lb cubes, 1lb bran, 1lb hay	2lb cubes, 1lb bran, 2lb hay

after a small feed of 1-1.5kg (2-3lb), but after a full feed no strenuous work should be done for 1½ hours.

7 Water before feeding.
8 Always use clean feeding utensils. The trough or manger, bucket, pan or feeding bowl must be kept clean; any remains of the previous feed must be removed before a fresh feed is given.

Good feeding is an acquired skill; it demands experience and a close interest in the animals, as each individual will have varying requirements. Some animals look well on very little feed and become too excitable if fed any more; others need as much feed as they will take, to maintain their energy and condition. Although there can be no absolute rules about quantities to feed, the following table does provide a rough guide, but it must

be used in conjunction with continual observation so that any changes in condition or performance can be noted at an early stage, and the feed adjusted accordingly.

Specimen diets
NB These are for horses with a sensible temperament. If the animal becomes unmanageable, substitute cubes for oats, or turn him out to grass for a few hours each day, or do both.

In the field
For owners of horses turned out in pastures, the usual problem is when to start feeding hay in the autumn and when to stop in the spring. But so much depends on the extent and quality of the available grazing; there can be no hard and fast rules. Weather is also a factor. During a mild winter, the grass will continue to grow and will contain some nutritive value, right up to the end of the year. The wisest plan is to start offering hay in late autumn but discontinue for a while if the hay is ignored. By mid winter, however, a daily haynet will be necessary. Once the grass starts to grow again in spring, the horse should be encouraged to eat some hay; you may have to tie the animal up and give him a haynet for two or three hours each day. Too much rich grass eaten too quickly may cause colic or laminitis. By spring, it should be possible to stop giving hay.

Concentrates may be given at any time, if the horse is in work or losing condition. Ponies, however, are usually best kept on cubes. Oats often go to their heads, turning them into unruly beasts.

The feed should be taken to the field at the same time each day to avoid any impatient fretting, which can impair the digestion.

Watering
This is as important as feed to a horse. Although the animal could stay alive for about a month without food, it would die in about a week if deprived of water. As a

5.00pm	8.00pm
3lb oats, 1lb bran, linseed jelly, roots, chaff	4lb oats, 1lb bran, chaff, 7lb hay
2lb oats, 1lb bran, linseed jelly, roots, chaff	3lb oats, 1lb bran, chaff, 6lb hay
2lb oats, 1lb bran, chaff	2lb oats, 1lb cubes, 1lb bran, 6lb hay
3lb oats, 1lb cubes, 1lb bran, chaff	3lb oats, 1lb cubes, 1lb bran, chaff 7lb hay
2lb oats, 1lb cubes, 1lb bran, roots, 6lb hay	
1lb oats, 2lb bran, chaff, 1lb carrots, 5lb hay	

general rule, water should be offered to horses before a meal and after exercise; watering on a full stomach, or immediately before energetic work, may cause pain and distress. Some horses, however, seem to like the opportunity of taking a light drink after a feed, and as long as they have been able to drink deeply beforehand, this should do no harm.

Watering in the stable
In the stable, water is usually contained in a bucket, which can be emptied and refilled four or five times a day. It should be placed in a corner away from the manger and haynet, so that it cannot become contaminated by loose hay or spilt feed. A bucket-holder will prevent it from being knocked over. Alternatively, an automatic

drinking bowl may be fitted in the box; the bowl should be checked regularly, however, to ensure that the mechanism is working and has not become clogged. Problems are especially likely to arise in cold weather when the supply pipes may freeze solid.

Watering in the field
Far less control over a horse's

drinking habits is possible in a field, but here the animal will most probably conform to the routine followed by horses in the wild, drinking at morning and evening but rarely in between.

A pastured (grass-kept) horse is visited less often than a stabled one, however, and it is easy to forget to check the water container at every visit. If the field possesses a running stream or an automatic water trough, fresh water will always be available. A running stream is the best watering system, provided that the ground bordering it is sound and that neither the ground nor the bed of the stream is composed of boulders or thick mud. A stagnant pond is better fenced off.

Automatic troughs draw water from pipes, with the supply being controlled by a ballcock and valve mechanism or a stop cock. The troughs should be situated in the open, away from hedges or over-hanging trees, so that several horses can drink at the same time and falling leaves will not pollute the water. If no other source is available, water must be supplied manually, by means of a hose or buckets. An old bath makes an adequate container, but it should be cleaned regularly and should be boxed in to prevent any sharp rim from injuring the horse. Buckets by themselves are unsatisfactory as they hold little water and are easily knocked over. A horse may drink as much as eight gallons during a day, so capacity is an important factor to consider.

In freezing weather, ice on the surface of the water must be frequently broken and removed. During a prolonged frost, water in the trough may freeze solid; in these circumstances, carrying water in buckets will be the only means of ensuring that your horse has enough to drink.

Left: A horse and foal enjoying excellent conditions: a large paddock with a stout post and rail fence and a sensible water trough supplied from a piped water system.

The purpose of grooming

First and foremost, grooming keeps a horse clean. It also massages, stimulates circulation of the blood and lymph, and tones up the muscles. Thus, grooming is a means of preventing disease (especially of the skin), of maintaining condition, and of improving appearance. For the horse in the stable, deprived of a natural life, daily grooming is essential to his well-being.

The grooming routine

Brief grooming, or quartering, is a five- or ten-minute grooming before a stable horse is worked. The feet are picked out and stable marks removed with a dandy brush or, if necessary, a damp sponge. The mane and tail are brushed with a body brush and put in place with a water brush. The eyes, muzzle and dock are sponged.

Grooming after exercise

When the horse returns to the stable after exercise the feet, if muddy, should be washed and then picked out. Any dry sweat marks may be removed with a dandy or body brush, but not until the coat is completely dry. If the horse is hot or wet, he may need to be sponged down before being dried off.

Thorough grooming (strapping)

Thorough grooming is the hardest part of the horse's routine; the best effects will be achieved only by 'elbow grease'.

Start with the dandy brush, to remove mud and sweat marks. This can be done only if the dirt has dried. Although it is possible to sponge marks off, it can lead to chapping and sores unless the area is dried adequately afterwards.

The field-kept horse stimulates his circulation by moving around, and the grease in his coat acts as a natural waterproofing agent. Because a horse kept in the stable has lost both these safeguards, it is best to avoid wetting the coat.

Brush off dirt wherever possible.

The real hard work starts with application of the body brush. The bristles must be driven through the horse's coat, beginning at the neck on the near side, to remove all the dirt and dried sweat. Stand far enough away from the horse to get your weight behind the brush. More force can be put into the task if the brush is held in the left hand on the nearside and the right hand on the offside. With a strong, circular motion, work the brush from the neck along the body, occasionally cleaning the brush with the curry comb. The belly, the flanks and the area between the forelegs should be covered. When grooming the hind legs, it is best to stand as close as possible at the side (not behind), so as to feel and see more easily if the horse is about to kick or move.

The head, especially around the eyes and ears, is a very sensitive area; use the brush gently but firmly. A dandy brush must never be used on the head. The mane and tail should be groomed into place and the hairs separated with the body brush. A dampened water brush can then be applied to keep the mane lying over. The tail can be bandaged to keep it in the correct shape.

The dock, eyes and nostrils should then be cleaned with the sponge, and the finishing touch is to wipe the horse over with a damp stable rubber.

A good grooming, however, should include some wisping, which both develops and hardens the muscles and stimulates the circulation. To be effective the dampened wisp must be brought down with some force on the horse to follow the lie of the hair. Aim for a rhythmical pattern of lift, down, thump and along. This wisping should be done in the regions of the muscles, ie, the shoulders and neck; the head, loins, belly and legs should not be wisped.

Setting fair (touch-ups)

Most horses have an additional

blanket or thicker rug put on them at the end of the day. This is a good opportunity to give them a quick brush-over and wisping.

The standard grooming kit (Below)
 1 *Stable rubber (for polishing)*
 2 *Sponge*
 3 *Large mane comb*
 4 *Sweat scraper*
 5 *Hoof pick*
 6 *Small mane comb*
 7 *Curry comb*
 8 *Grooming kit bag*
 9 *Water brush*
10 *Dandy brush*
11 *Body brush*

To make a wisp
Twist some dampened hay into a rope of about 2m (7ft). At one end, arrange the rope into two loops, one slightly longer than the other. Twist each loop in turn under the rest of the rope, until there is none left. To finish, twist the end of the rope through the end of each loop and tuck in (see diagram on page 104).

To pick out the feet
Stand beside the horse's shoulder or hindquarters. Run the hand down the back of the leg towards the hoof, which the average animal

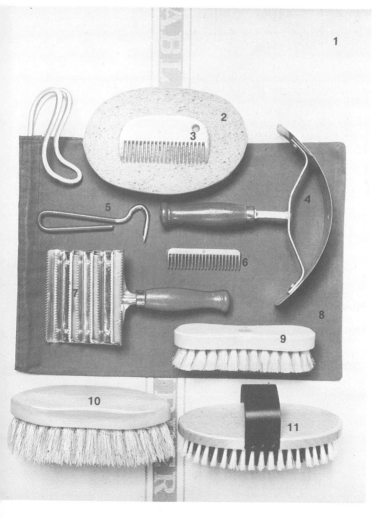

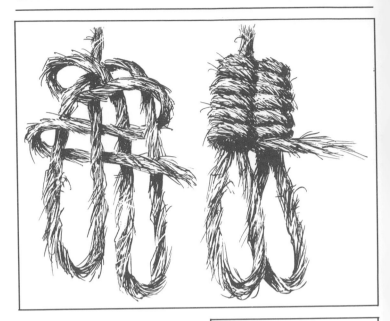

Above: Make a wisp from twisted hay by forming two loops and pulling tight as shown here.
Right: Picking out the hoof. With short strokes work towards the toe, removing all mud, dirt and stones.

will then pick up. If he does not, push on the shoulder or hind-quarters to make him transfer his weight to the other leg and pinch the back of the leg with the hand. When the leg is lifted, hold it firmly around the coronet and pick out the hoof with a blunt-ended hoof pick, starting from the heel.

The grass-kept horse

Only limited grooming is needed for animals living outside. The grease and dandruff in the coat help to waterproof the hair and keep the animal warm; it is inadvisable, therefore, to clean a grass-kept horse too vigorously, in case his natural means of protection is removed.

Grooming should be limited to picking out his feet, removing mud with a dandy brush or rubber curry comb, brushing mane and tail with a body brush, laying the mane with a water brush, and finally sponging the muzzle, eyes and dock.

The grooming machine

Grooming machines (vacuum cleaners) are a great help in busy stables. They must, however, be operated intelligently; it is easy to frighten a horse and to damage the machine. It is inadvisable to groom with them every day — normal practice is to use them once or twice a week. On the other days, the horse can be groomed by hand, a process that usually takes much less time than a normal grooming because so much of the grease and dirt has been removed from the horse's coat by the machine on the preceding day.

Removal of all or part of a thick coat is needed for horses in hard, regular work. Clipping both prevents excessive sweating and enables the horse to dry quickly afterwards. It also makes him look trim and neat, although this is not the main reason for clipping.

The first clip of the season is carried out as soon as the new winter coat is well established, usually in the autumn. The first sign that the winter coat is on the way is the disappearance of the high gloss of summer. Suddenly, the coat feels more woolly beneath the fingers as the short hairs thicken, the top hairs grow longer and the finer summer hairs begin to fall out. At work the horse sweats more easily.

Electrically operated clippers are the most efficient means of removing the coat. They are quick, easy to use after some practice and, when oiled during the cut and sharpened at intervals, give a satisfactory clip. Hand-operated clippers are good, but rather tiring to use.

Types of clip
The extent of the clipping should depend on the work the horse will be expected to do, and on how much he sweats.

A full clip
This clip is one in which all the hair is removed from the head (except muzzle and ears), neck, body and legs of the horse. This is used on heavily coated animals, on whom the hair on the legs is ugly and so thick that it becomes difficult to dry.

The hunter clip
This leaves hair on the legs as far as the elbow and top of the thighs. This protects the horse against gorse, thorns and other matter encountered in cross-country riding, and reduces the risk of heels cracking. Sometimes, a patch of hair is left on the back under the saddle to help stop rubbing, but if the hair is excessively thick it is best removed to prevent excessive sweating.

The blanket clip
This leaves most of the body hair (in the shape of a blanket) and all the leg hair. The head, neck, belly, part of the thighs and a thin strip up the back of the quarters are clipped. It is used in particular for Thoroughbreds who, because of their fine coats, do not need to have so much removed to reduce the sweating.

The trace-high clip
The briefest clip of all, this removes hair only from the belly, chest, and part of the thighs and up the back of the quarters. A strip on the underside of the neck is also sometimes removed. The trace-

Below: Clipping styles. The hunter clip (left) and blanket clip (right).

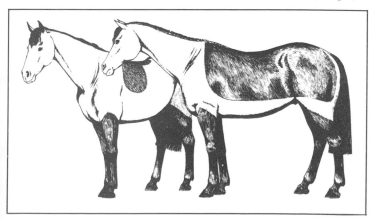

high clip is popular for horses that are to be kept out during the winter but will be hunted during winter holidays; it prevents excessive sweating without removing any of the animal's protection against the weather.

How to clip

Clipping takes time and patience. An assistant should be available to help if required.

The horse's coat should be as dry and well-groomed as possible. The most important factor is not to upset the animal. Before the clip is started, the assistant should hold the horse, talk to him, pat him, and be reassuring. If the horse becomes restless when the ticklish areas (for instance, the belly) are being clipped, the assistant can lift one of the horse's legs to prevent him from moving around.

Start clipping in the areas that are least ticklish and sensitive, such as the shoulder—not the head, groin or belly.

Ensure that the clippers do not overheat, and that the blades are sharp and do not pull the hairs; clippers must be run flat along the skin and not dug into the horse, and they should be guided, not pushed, against the lie of the coat.

Do not clip into the sides of the mane or the root of the tail, or inside the ears. The backs of the tendon and fetlock are usually better dealt with by scissors and comb. The comb and scissors should be moved upward against the hair, in the same way as a professional hairdresser trims human hair.

Care of a clipped horse

The clipped horse needs a blanket to compensate for the loss of his thick coat. A blanket made of jute or hemp and lined with wool is used in most cases, with or without an additional blanket underneath. A recent innovation in the UK is a quilted rug, which is warm and light and can be used in place of the night rug and blanket.

Right: How to braid the mane.

Mane- and tail-pulling

These tasks are forgotten by many horse owners, who perhaps worry that they may do a poor job and produce more problems than they solve. But a well-pulled mane and tail give a good appearance and, in the case of the mane, make it easier to plait for hunting or showing.

Pulling thin hair from the mane makes the ends even (scissors should never be used) and helps it to lie flat. The task is best carried out when the horse is warm and the pores of the skin are open so that hairs will come out easily and without discomfort. Always remove the hairs from the underside of the mane, and never take out more than a few hairs with each pull. It is best to do a little each day rather than keep going for a long time, which could make the animal sore.

Tail-pulling means removing (never with scissors) the short, bushy hairs from the top of the tail. It is done solely to give a neat appearance. It should not be carried out on grass-kept animals, who need the short hairs at the top of the tail to protect the region around the dock.

Mane- and tail-braiding (plaiting)

These give the final touch to the overall show-ring appearance of a horse, and show off his neck and quarters to best advantage. Braiding is also a useful means of making an unruly mane lie flat on the correct side.

Braiding the mane

The mane should be braided on the morning of the show, and the braids must be taken out at the end of the show to avoid damaging the hair by splitting or tearing.

Braids are made from withers to forelock, usually about a mane-comb's length apart. There should be an uneven number of braids up the length of the neck.

The hair is first damped with a water brush and divided into sections. Each section in turn is then braided so that the top of the braid is tight against the roots of the hair. The end is then secured, by means of a needle and thread passed through the plait and wound tightly around it, before being folded under and stitched to the braid about half way up. The resulting loop is then rolled up tightly until it forms a knob close to the poll, where it is stitched firmly in place. Sharp-pointed embroidery scissors are needed to remove the stitches at the end of the day.

Braiding with rubber bands is a quicker method, but it is difficult to achieve such a smart result as that given by needle and thread. The hair is braided in the same manner and a rubber band is looped around the long braid several times. The end is then turned up into the desired position and the band looped around the entire braid to make it secure.

Tail braiding

Tail braiding is carried out in a similar manner, starting at the top of the tail, braiding down the centre and drawing in the side hairs on the way. When the braid is two thirds of the way down the tail bone, start leaving out the side hairs. Continue the braid, using only the centre hairs. The end of the braid should be stitched and bound securely with needle and thread, doubled under and attached to the point where the braiding of the side hairs ends.

Below: How to braid the tail.

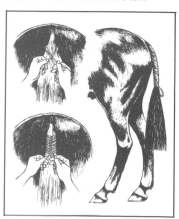

A stabled horse must be regularly exercised. Otherwise he runs the risk of swollen legs, azoturia and colic, and is also likely to show spirited behaviour when ridden. One rest day a week is acceptable, but on the evening before this it is advisable to give a laxative bran mash.

The amount of exercise given to the horse will depend on his type (Thoroughbreds need more than ponies), the type of work being prepared for (three-day eventers

Below: Almost ready for exercise. The horse is tacked up, the Yorkshire boots are in place on the hind legs and the girl is just buckling up the brushing boots, with the straps pointing towards the hind legs.

need more than hacks), the amount of energy food the animal is receiving (horses being given large quantities of oats need more than those on pellets [cubes]), and his fitness (a horse that has been in work for only a week requires less than one that is ready to go hunting).

Preparation for exercise
Exercise should not take place until at least one and a half hours after a large feed, or one hour after a small one. It is also advisable to take the hay away one hour before exercise, as a horse or pony stuffed full of hay will find breathing more difficult. In the case of a horse about to be put to fast work, this precaution is essential, and must be observed.

When ready to exercise the horse, he should be tied up and quartered (see Grooming above) before tacking up. If boots or bandages are worn, these should be put on first. Yorkshire boots are used if the horse brushes his hind fetlocks; they are attached firmly just above the fetlock so that they cannot slip down. Brushing boots are used on the forelegs, and are advisable on all valuable horses as they reduce the likelihood of injuries or splints being caused by blows or brushing. The brushing boots should be put on with the ends of the straps pointing towards the hind legs. The bottom strap should be done up first, to stop the boot slipping down, and the straps should be tight enough to stop the boot passing over the fetlock joint.

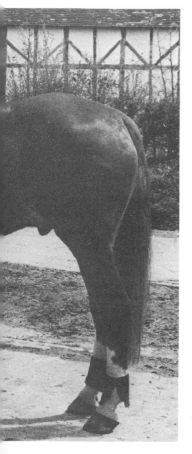

Some horse owners use exercise bandages, either because they like the additional protection these provide, or because the horse has weak tendons that need support. Others argue that this regular support to the leg prevents it hardening up to withstand the strain. Bandages need to be put on very carefully, because if they are too tight they can cause damage and if too loose they will slip. They should be applied over a layer of tissue or gamgee and should be neither so high nor so low as to interfere with the action of the joints. They should be applied firmly in the manner shown (see diagram). The tapes should be knotted in a bow at the side of the leg; not at the front or at the back, where they might interfere with the bone or the tendon. Ends of tapes should be tucked in.

If the exercise includes jumping, all but small ponies should wear over-reach boots, which are worn just above the hoof. Some varieties of these boots can be buckled into position, but many have no buckles and have to be pulled on. It is best to start by turning them inside out. The foot is then picked up and rested on the attendant's knees while the over-reach boot is held by the broader rim and pulled over the hoof. When the narrower rim is over the hoof, the boot can be turned the right way out, to hang in the correct place.

After all the necessary clothing protecting the legs is in position, the saddle and martingales, and finally the bridle, can be put on.

The horse is then ready, but in stables where turnout is considered important, hoof oil is put on the feet to add a finishing touch to his appearance.

Care after exercise
Ideally the horse's exercise should end with a walk so that he returns to the stable cool and relaxed. The bridle can then be taken off, and the horse can be tied up before the saddle and leg clothing are removed. The animal should then be inspected for any injuries and

feet picked out to clear them of mud and to ensure that no stones or foreign bodies are lodged in them. The feet may be washed if muddy, but try not to get the heels wet; if this is unavoidable, take care to dry them out, or cracked heels may develop.

Depending on the stable routine, the exercised horse may be strapped immediately or merely have the saddle and bridle sweat marks brushed or sponged off before being rugged up. In the latter case the strapping can be done at a more convenient time. This is more usual, because the horse is so often warm after exercise, and a sticky sweaty coat cannot be groomed properly.

Occasionally the horse cannot be returned to the stable dry and relaxed — for instance, if his coat has been soaked by rain. In this case it is better to trot the animal back to the stable so that he is warm on arrival. Untack the horse as before and rub him down with straw, a stable rubber or an old towel. When he is reasonably dry put a cooler (sweat sheet) on or cover his back with straw. A blanket (night rug) can then be put on top, but it is advisable to turn it inside out so that the lining does not get damp. It is also best to fold the blanket back over the horse's shoulders so that the air can get to, and dry, the neck and shoulders. The vital area to keep warm is the back.

There are occasions, such as during strenuous work, or in a summer heatwave, when the horse gets very hot. Then he will need to be sponged down, preferably with buckets of lukewarm water. Some people advocate bathing him all over, whereas others just sponge the sweaty areas, fearing that too much water will take the grease out of the horse's coat and make him susceptible to chills. These objections are valid, but there is little danger if proper precautions are taken. The horse should not be bathed every day, and should be thoroughly dried before being returned to the stall or box.

The drying process starts (in the case of both a sponge and a washdown) with the sweat scraper. This is run firmly along the coat in the direction of the lay of the hair to squeeze out the water. In order to be effective the edge of the sweat scraper should be relatively sharp, and therefore should not be used on sensitive areas such as the head.

After being scraped the horse may be rubbed down. Ideally a cooler or sweat sheet should be put on, and the horse led around until dry. On returning to the stable it is a wise precaution to leave the cooler or sweat sheet on, and to put the blanket (night rug) over it, folded back and upside down.

A horse that has been hunted or worked in competitions will need special attention when he returns to his stable. Colic or chills may develop unless this treatment is

thorough. Firstly the horse should be given a drink of warm water. Then, if he likes to roll, turn him loose in a thickly bedded stable for a few minutes. Do not leave the horse, however, if he stands still and does not roll, for he must be kept warm.

Tie the horse and remove sweat and wet mud with a damp sponge. Rug him up with a cooler or sweat sheet or straw under a folded-back blanket (rug) and inspect him for any injuries. If there is dry mud on the legs, brush this off; any that remains can be washed off as long as the legs are dried immediately afterwards. The feet can then be picked out and if necessary washed, but the heels must be dried.

If his coat is not sticky with sweat, the horse can be unrugged for a few minutes and given a quick going-over with the body brush. Finally, he should be given a good

warm bran mash and left to rest. Check later to ensure that the horse has eaten up and is warm enough, but has not started to sweat. If he has started to sweat he should be rubbed down and walked around. To find out if he is cold, feel his ears. If they are not warm at the base, remedies are needed. The ears themselves should be rubbed and more blankets should be put on the horse.

Some horse-keepers think they can keep their horse warmer and happier by using stable bandages.

Below: Washing down after hard exercise. The horse has been sponged down all over and the girl is using the seat scraper to remove as much of the water and sweat as possible. After a sponge down and scrape the horse should be rubbed down and led around until he is dry. Put on a cooler to prevent chills.

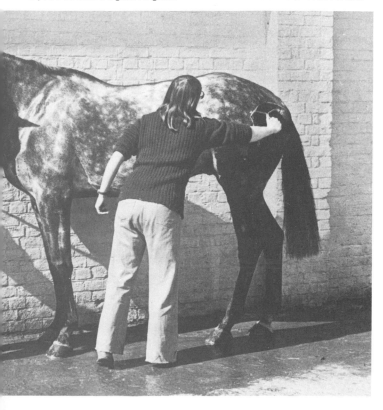

In order to make the most of a rally, competition or hunt, it is vital to plan the preparations. If this is not done, everything may be ruined by arriving too late, getting into a panic or forgetting some vital piece of equipment. But these preparations are fun, for almost everyone enjoys the excitement of anticipating the sport ahead, whether that sport is to be in the hunting field, in the competition arena or with the Pony Club. It is no hardship, therefore, to put aside time on the preceding days to organize a timetable, and to prepare the equipment, the horse and the rider.

The arrangements for transportation

The method of travel should be planned well in advance. If the event is to take place up to 16km (10 miles) away, it should be possible to hack, and an average fit horse should walk and trot the distance at 10kph (6mph). An animal that is off grass, however, should be kept to the walk as much as possible, which will reduce the average speed by about 3kph (2mph).

If the distance is too far to be hacked, those without transport will have to hire a trailer or lorry and driver, hire a trailer that they can tow behind their own car, or persuade friends to collect the horse. Whichever method is decided upon, it must be arranged well ahead of the event.

Those with their own transportation may enjoy the independence, but it does entail more work. The fuel tank, tyre pressures, and condition of the vehicle all need to be checked, in addition to preparing accommodation for the horse. The travelling compartment must be clean, and a haynet hung up to keep the animal happy on the journey. If he is expected to work hard soon after arrival, though, the filled haynet should be put out of reach until the work has been done. The vehicle should then be loaded with all the equipment needed at the rally, show or meet.

Preparation of tack and clothing

Those who travel to many events find it best to list all the necessary equipment and to keep the list in the tack room, where each item can be checked off as it is loaded into the transport. This list will vary according to the type of activity, and those who are hacking to a rally or meet do not need one at all, for nothing is needed other than the tack the horse wears. The only important thing is that the tack is cleaned the day before and inspected to make sure that it is in good order.

For those going by trailer or lorry the list expands to include a fork, shovel and brush to keep the transport clean; a haynet for the journey; a feed if the horse is to be away for a long time; a blanket (day rug) or sheet and bandages, for travelling; a cooler or sweat sheet to place under the rugs to help the horse cool down if he gets hot; a spare halter or headcollar in case one gets broken; water in a container, and a bucket from which to drink it.

If going hunting, and if the journey is not too long, it is probably easiest to transport the horse or pony tacked up, with a rug over the top of the saddle and a tail bandage to prevent any rubbing. If going to a competition, as the animal is usually more valuable and the journey longer, special clothing for travelling may be used to give the best possible protection (see Transportation below). The competition horse will also need additional equipment when he arrives, and most seasoned travellers to competitions have trunks in which to keep it. A full grooming kit will be needed; studs if the going is likely to be slippery; brushing, Yorkshire and over-reach boots, and exercise bandages, as necessary. Then there is the saddlery, which can include a line and cavesson for lungeing to get some of the spirits out of over-fresh or excitable horses. A first-aid box should be part of the kit (see page 171), and when the going is very hard this can include a cooling wash to be applied to the legs after work. A useful luxury is a mackintosh sheet to keep the horse dry in heavy rain.

Preparation of the rider

It is a tradition in the horse world to pay great attention to the turnout of the rider. A handsome effect, it is thought, gives horse and rider a feeling of pride that makes them perform just a little bit better. Although expensive and beautifully fitting clothes can be an advantage, the most valued factor is cleanliness. Gleaming boots, brushed jackets and hats and clean breeches make rack or 'off the peg' equipment look just as good as the custom-made or tailored items, and so, before any event, time must be set aside for polishing boots and washing and brushing clothes.

Clothes are not the only key to smartness; hair is often overlooked. Girls should experiment to find out how their hair can be arranged for the most becoming and tidy effect. The coiffure should be fastened securely, for overhanging branches and hedges can play havoc with any tresses that are precariously arranged. Men should consider a short hair style.

The dress for children

under about 16 years can be the same for all activities. It consists of:
A riding crop.
Jodhpur boots (brown with a tweed jacket, or black with a black or blue jacket).
Spurs – but only for lazy ponies with good riders.
Jodhpurs, although children sometimes prefer breeches and top boots.
A white shirt.
A tie – if the child is a member, the Pony Club tie may be worn.
A tie pin to keep the tie from blowing around.
A waistcoat or V-necked sweater in cold weather.
A tweed jacket (although a black or blue coat may be used for smart occasions).
A riding cap (or a derby [bowler]) for hunting.
Gloves.

The riding attire for older riders

should vary according to the activity, with well-kept clothes presenting a smart, neat turnout.
Hunting has the strongest traditions with regard to dress, but

Below: Members of the hunt in traditional dress, a style known throughout the world.

certain modernizations are becoming acceptable. For instance, although a hunting whip is correct, more and more people carry a crop in the hunting field. Top boots are more normal than jodhpur boots, but modern manufacturers make such good rubber versions (which can be polished) that there is no need to buy expensive leather ones. Spurs should be worn, but a rider with a skittish animal would probably be forgiven for leaving them off. Jodhpurs may be worn, but breeches are more acceptable and are usually cheaper. It is best to buy thick ones; skimpy nylon breeches will not be warm enough. The hunting shirt is made of wool or silk, and is thus warmer than a normal shirt; it has no collar, which makes it easier to wear the hunting tie (stock). The stock can be bought ready tied but it takes only a little study and practice to tie one's own. An ordinary shirt and tie may be worn with a tweed jacket. The coat can be tweed, but it is smarter to wear black or blue. Traditionally, only the hunt servants and farmers had the right to wear a derby (bowler) or top hat: fewer and fewer hunts, however, are enforcing this rule. Gloves are essential for all but the very tough in winter time. When in doubt what to wear, ask the Master or Honorary Secretary's advice.

In competitions the dress was originally based on what was acceptable in the hunting field, but practical variations have crept in. Breeches, coats and shirts are now more lightweight, as competitors do not have to wait about for long periods in the cold and rain. The tie worn with a blue, black or red coat is rarely a stock, simply a white or blue tie. Most types of spurs and crops are accepted and the hat is normally a hunting cap.

In dressage those in the higher echelons (Prix St Georges and above) are expected to wear top hats and tail coats.

In the cross-country phase of eventing the emphasis is on protection, so crash helmets are worn. Coats are replaced by high-necked sweaters or shirts.

Riders competing in Saddle-horse classes wear saddle suits consisting of a long-skirted jacket and bell-bottomed (Kentucky) jodhpurs of the same material and colour, and occasionally a matching vest (waistcoat). Other items are a derby (bowler) or soft hat, shirt and tie, and jodhpur boots. More conservative colours are preferred for eventing classes.

Western Division riders must wear a Western-style hat, a long-sleeved shirt, and cowboy boots. The choice of trousers is left to the competitor, although most people wear either slim-cut frontier pants or jeans. Chaps should be worn.

Hunting dress *(Below)*
1 *Hunt cap*
2 *Stock (tie)*
3 *Hunt coat*
4 *Gloves*
5 *Breeches*
6 *Whip (or crop)*
7 *Garter straps*
8 *Top boots*

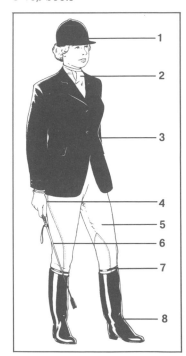

Preparation of the horse

Little can be done to prepare the horse the day before an event other than giving him an extra good grooming, and washing his mane and tail, and even this might have to be done again if they are of a light colour and get stained during the night.

If the horse is normally kept at grass, bring him in the night before if possible. This will help to keep him cleaner and save time in the morning. It is on the day of the show that so much of the work has to be done, and the vital factor is that it starts early enough to avoid panic and rush.

The initial work should consist of the normal stable routine: watering, feeding and mucking out. After this the horse can be groomed, and (if there is time) given as good a strapping as possible. For most events the mane must be braided (plaited) and the tail bandaged.

The final preparations will depend on the intended programme. Horses for rallies, and hunters, can be saddled up. Competition horses can have their legs bandaged (see page 146), and a blanket (day rug) or sheet put on for travelling.

After all this, it is to be hoped that there will be time to set things right for the return, ensuring that the mash can be prepared easily, that the horse's bed is clean and that water and hay are ready.

The preparations over, it is at last time for the start of the action.

Saddle-horse dress (Below)
1 *Derby*
2 *Tie*
3 *Saddle coat*
4 *Gloves*
5 *Whip*
6 *Kentucky jodhpurs*
7 *Jodhpur boots*

Western riding dress (Below)
1 *Western hat*
2 *Western style shirt*
3 *Gloves*
4 *Lasso*
5 *Chaps (Worn over jeans or slim-cut frontier pants)*
6 *Cowboy boots*

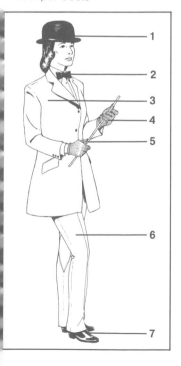

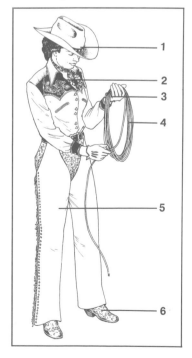

Barely 150 years ago, the only means of travelling any distance by land was on horseback. Now ironically, except on long-distance rides, mounted expeditions or pony treks, the last method to be considered for getting a horse from A to B is on his own legs. Today, horses travel by trailer, horse-box, plane, or even occasionally by ship. A few years ago trains could have been added to the list, but in most countries it is becoming less and less popular as a means of transporting horses, and in the UK the rolling stock of British Rail no longer includes a horse-wagon.

The journey

Fortunately, most horses travel well, and appear to suffer no ill effects from a long journey. The interior of a trailer or horse-box is well padded and designed to give the animal support against jolting and swaying when the vehicle is under way. A haynet should be all that is necessary to keep the horse on the move but, if desired, a light feed may be given in a nosebag.

If the journey is to take several hours, arrangements should be made for occasional stops so that

Below: This horse has been dressed for travelling. He is wearing a halter (headcollar), day rug, roller with felt pad attached, knee caps, travelling bandages, hock boots and a tail bandage.

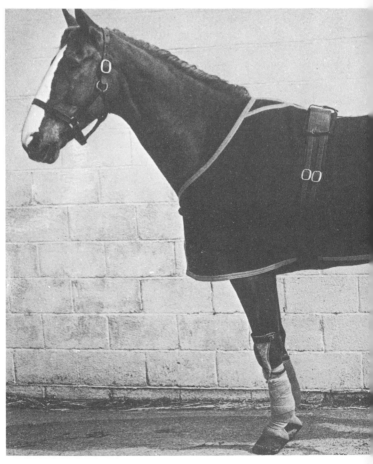

the horse can be watered. He can also be unloaded and walked around to ease any stiffness. The horse will appreciate the chance to graze quietly for 20 minutes or so. If the journey is to last more than about four hours, the diet should be fairly light during the 24 hours before departure, with the oat ration reduced by half.

Clothing

Valuable animals should be equipped with protective clothing. Flannel or wool travelling bandages should always be worn, as should a tail guard or tail bandage to stop the top of the tail being rubbed. On long journeys or for bad travellers, knee caps and hock boots are advisable to protect

these highly susceptible joints. On an air journey, when the horse may have to pass under a low beam or doorway, a poll pad is desirable to guard against injury to the top of the head. If no poll pad is available, cotton wool or foam rubber, wrapped around the headpiece of the halter or head-collar and held in place by a stable bandage, will serve instead.

All horses should wear a well-fitting halter. Blankets or rugs are necessary only if the horse is accustomed to wearing one in the stable. On a hot day, a cooler (sweat sheet) or a summer sheet is advisable.

Loading

Loading should present no problems as long as the horse has been carefully loaded and driven in the past. But it is very easy to frighten an animal by not being patient and thoughtful when first getting him accustomed to being loaded, and by driving too fast, especially before he has learned to balance himself with the strange movement. Horses must be driven smoothly and steadily, so that they are not swung off their feet when the vehicle goes around corners, or jolted backwards and forwards by heavy braking and acceleration.

If there is any possibility of a horse being a 'shy loader', or if he is travelling for the first time, the timetable should allow for delays.

The person leading a horse into the transport should walk confidently ahead, and should not look behind and pull. Staring at the horse tends to put him off going forward. Any helpers should be behind the horse.

Apart from thoughtless driving and handling, one of the main reasons for reluctance to load is fear of the ramp, which reverberates when struck by the horse's hoof. Straw may be liberally spread on it to deaden the sound, and a non-slip mat is an advantage. A reluctant traveller will sometimes enter the trailer or horse-box quite readily if he can follow a stable companion, or a feed bucket containing a few oats may tempt a greedy one. If all else fails, you may have to resort to ropes attached to the rails of the ramp and crossed behind the horse just above his hocks. Two assistants are needed to hold the loose ends of the ropes, and to tighten them as the horse and his handler approach the ramp. If ropes are not available, the linked arms of the two assistants can be used to push against the horse's rump to help loading.

Forms of road transport

Those who do not transport their horses very often may prefer to hire the services of professional transporters. Although this is relatively expensive, there are enormous benefits. The drivers are experienced in loading and driving, and the horse owner avoids the expense and worry of maintaining personal transport.

But as journeys become more frequent, it becomes inconvenient to have to rely on others. Most horse owners start by buying a trailer. These come in various sizes and can be towed behind any powerful car or jeep, which means that no special lorry license is needed. In the USA these trailers have been developed into a very sophisticated method of horse transportation, but the versions in the UK are more primitive and have disadvantages. They must be driven slowly or the trailer starts to sway, and even the largest is not suitable to carry more than two medium-sized horses.

So, particularly in the UK, horse-boxes are more popular than trailers with people who have to transport their horses for long distances. In them the horses enjoy a smoother ride, but the driver does need to be experienced to manage such a large vehicle. Today most governments require drivers to take special heavy goods vehicle tests before a license is granted to drive these vehicles.

Air travel

Though more expensive than sea travel, air travel is becoming a much more usual means of taking horses abroad. Racehorses going abroad to race are carried in freight planes. These are especially chartered by blood-stock agencies, who normally make all arrangements, including the supply of trained grooms to attend the horses on their journey. It is also possible to make private arrangements with air-ferry companies.

Travelling abroad

All over the world there are strict controls regarding the import and export of horses, and this includes temporary visits to a foreign country for races or competitions. Anyone contemplating taking a horse abroad should contact the appropriate government department, and an agent who specializes in the transport of horses, for accurate and up-to-date advice about documents required (ie, import/export license and veterinary certificates).

The major purpose of these restrictions is to prevent the spread of contagious diseases. South Africa is one country that has these precautions. Europeans, fearful that African horse-sickness could be introduced into their territory, have banned the import of horses from South Africa.

Insurance when travelling

Special insurance policies are available to cover animals against transportation risks, either during a specific journey or for a period of time, for instance during the show season. Most professional transporters, however, are covered against the risk of damaging horses that are travelling in their vehicles.

To what extent you insure a horse against accidental injury may depend on the value of the animal. More details of insurance policies are given on page 180.

Above: A horse being unloaded in the correct way — at a steady pace.
Left: A horse loading willingly. The assistant walks confidently by his side without pulling him or looking back at him.

The blacksmith is a very important person in a horse's life, for a good smith can correct certain faults of conformation, improve the condition of the feet and prevent weaknesses from developing. A bad one can ruin a horse for life.

The choice of blacksmith must, therefore, be made with care. Few places these days have a forge, and more often the blacksmith has to come to the horse, rather than wait for his clients to visit him. Conversely, the necessity of going outside the immediate locality in search of a smith may offer a choice of two or three of them. The best method of selection is to find out which blacksmith visits neighbouring horses and arrange for your own horse to be shod at the same time.

Hot and cold shoeing

The lack of forges has led to an increase in cold shoeing. This is the system whereby a smith measures a horse's feet, and makes a set of shoes at his forge, then fits them cold. At this stage, he cannot make any further adjustment to the shoes; so they are unlikely to be as good a fit as with hot shoeing. In hot shoeing, the shoe is heated on the spot. It is then hammered into shape and placed on the foot for a few seconds to char a brown rim on the hoof. The shoe can then be altered if necessary, and so can the hoof; for an incomplete brown rim indicates that there is some space between the shoe and the hoof. The bearing surface of the hoof should be made level by rasping it before attaching the shoe.

The shoe

The horseshoe has changed little in style since the first iron shoe was nailed by a Celtic horseman to his horse's hoof nearly 2,000 years ago, but it has undergone certain refinements. Most shoes are now fullered (that is, they have a groove on the underside to improve grip with the ground). Most, too, are concave, so that they are narrower on the ground surface than above. This makes the shoe lighter and less likely to be pulled off in sticky ground.

Clips help to keep the shoe in place. These are small triangular extensions of the outer edge of the shoe that fit into the wall of the hoof. It is usual to have one clip on each fore shoe, and two clips on each hind shoe (one on each side). Central clips are rare on hind shoes, for without them there is less risk of the metal causing an over-reach.

Grip is an important requirement of a shoe. A fullered surface helps, and there are other possible modifications. Calks or calkins can be forged on the heels of hind shoes by turning the ends of the shoe downward to provide a small projection. Even more grip can be

Below: A blacksmith checks a shoe against the hoof for a good fit.

obtained with the small mordax studs that the blacksmith can attach to the hind shoes. They are especially beneficial for horses that do a lot of roadwork (for instance, hunters and driving horses). The greatest grip of all is provided, however, by studs larger than the mordax versions. They are too large to leave in permanently, as they would make walking on hard road surfaces very awkward. Consequently, the smith prepares screw holes on the outer edge of the hind shoes, and sometimes on the fore shoes too. Studs can then be screwed into the holes as required for such activities as show-jumping.

A horseshoe should be held securely by nails that are hammered through the horny part of the foot until they emerge higher up, when their points are twisted off and the ends, known as clenches, are hammered down. A properly fitting shoe should not interfere in any way with the functions of the various parts of the foot.

The foot
It is important for keepers of horses to have at least an elementary understanding of the structure of the foot so that they can recognize if the work of the blacksmith is good or bad.

The inner core of the foot consists of three major bones: the lower section of the corner bone (short pastern); the coffin, or pedal, bone; and, situated between the wings of the pedal bone; the navicular bone. These bones are surrounded by very sensitive fleshy parts that, if pricked or damaged, will make a horse lame. These sensitive parts produce corresponding horny and insensitive structures that form the protective outer casing of the foot.

The wall
This is the horny insensitive structure seen when the foot is on the ground. It is comparable to our finger nails and, like them, is always growing. This growth is

downward, originating from the area of the coronary band. Some water is present in the horn, adding flexibility to this casing of the foot, and its evaporation is reduced by a thin layer of hard 'varnish' outside.

The wall is divided into three areas: the toe, which is at the front and is the highest section; the quarters, which are at the sides; and the heels, which are at the back where the wall curves inward to form the bars.

The horn of the wall is continuously growing. When the foot is unshod, the horn will wear down with friction, but when shoes are attached, it will start to spread after a few weeks and can eventually overlap the shoe, break away from the nail holes and possibly make the horse lame. The shoes must therefore be removed at regular intervals and the hoof pared into shape.

The sole
This protects the foot from injury from below. Although horny and insensitive, its outer layer grows from the sensitive area of the sole, which covers the under part of the

Underside of the foot *(Below)*
1 *Cleft of frog*
2 *Bar*
3 *Heel*
4 *White line*
5 *Wall*
6 *Point of the frog*
7 *Sole*
8 *Toe*

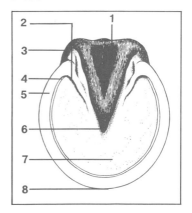

pedal bone. The outer layer is thin; it can very easily be pierced or damaged and the sensitive area made vulnerable.

The healthy sole is slightly concave to the ground. Dividing it and the wall is a white line, visible from below, which is a layer of soft horn. Its position is important, for it indicates to the smith the thickness of the wall and consequently how much room there is for the nails, which must never be allowed to penetrate the sole.

The frog

This is visible from below as a triangular area of horn at a lower level than the sole. The sensitive or fleshy frog is above it, inside the hoof, and like the sensitive sole, produces the horn of its insensitive area. The sections of the frog are made of relatively elastic material, providing the foot with both a shock absorber and a non-slip device. The heel meets the ground before the toe, so that it is this area that bears the brunt of the shock. For the frog to carry out this vital function it must be in contact with the ground. The smith, therefore, must never pare it back, but only remove any ragged ends. It is important, though, that the frog, like the sole, does not get any sharp objects lodged in it. It should therefore be picked out regularly with a hoof pick.

Reasons for shoeing

People sometimes wonder whether shoeing is strictly necessary, because a horse in the wild wears no shoes at all. As with additional feeding, the answer to this depends on the sort of work the animal has to do.

Plenty of work, part of it on solid surfaces such as roads, will wear the hoof down faster than it grows and lead to friction, soreness and finally lameness, as the softer parts of the foot have to take the weight. Another factor is climate; in the temperate zones of the Northern Hemisphere, the hard part of the foot tends to be comparatively soft. In Mediterranean countries, the Arab has traditionally gone unshod for centuries; but the atmosphere is drier there and hooves harder, so that the hoof wears more slowly and evenly.

Shoeing is not necessary on hardy animals doing light work on grass or in sandy areas, provided their feet are in good shape and regularly inspected and trimmed by the smith. If their hooves are brittle, however, with a tendency to crack or split, shoeing is essential and may be the only means of preventing lameness. For example, a horse with severe sandcrack (in which a crack in the hoof extends upward into the coronary and downward towards the bottom of the hoof) may be helped by the trimming of the foot and the use of a special corrective shoe to prevent pressure on the wall.

Checks to be made on a newly shod foot

1 The type of shoe should be suitable for the work required of the horse, and the weight of iron proportional to the size of the animal. Normally a horse's set weighs in the region of 2kg (4½lb), whereas a pony of about 12hh needs a set weighing just over 1kg (2¼lb).

2 The shoe should be made to fit the foot, not the foot made to fit the shoe (so not too much rasping and severe paring back of the hoof).

3 The length of the foot should have been reduced evenly at toe and heel.

4 The frog should be in contact with the ground.

5 An adequate number of nails should have been used, but not too many. The usual number is three on the inside and four on the outside.

6 The clenches should be neat, in line and the right distance up the wall.

7 There should be no space between shoe and foot.

8 The heels of the shoe should be neither too long nor too short.

9 It is important that the clip should fit well on each shoe.

Special types of shoe

Horses with conformation faults (such as a tendency to brush and injure the opposite leg) can be fitted with feather-edged shoes. The inner side of such a shoe is very much thinner than that of a normal shoe, so that it fits close in under the inside wall. Nails are used only around the toe and outer arm of the shoe.

Hunters out at pasture during the summer usually have their shoes removed and replaced by toe-clips. These small, half-size shoes, fitted only to the toe, prevent the hoof from cracking and encourage the frog to come into full contact with the ground.

Racehorses use two types of shoes: a light fullered concave shoe of mild steel for training, and a fullered, concave 'plate', usually of aluminium, for racing. A set of racehorse plates weighs only 250-500g (½-1lb) a set.

Great improvements have been made in recent years to the materials used for hoof pads. Various forms and shapes of plastics have been developed which, when placed between the shoe and the hoof, help to reduce jar. They are being used more and more for horses with foot or tendon problems and for horses that are required to jump on hard ground or to do much road work.

Indications that re-shoeing is necessary

1 Loose shoe.
2 'Cast' shoe (one that has been lost).
3 Shoe wearing thin.
4 Clenches rising and standing out from the wall.
5 Long foot and/or one that has lost its shape.

Depending on the amount of work a horse does, re-shoeing is usually necessary about once a month; either new shoes or 'removes' can be fitted. Removes are old shoes that, if not worn too thin, can be replaced after the foot has been trimmed.

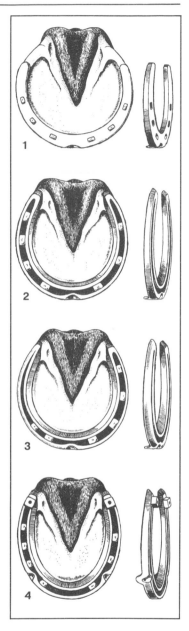

Types of horseshoe *(Above)*
1 *A half shoe fitted onto a fore foot.*
2 *A fullered fore shoe with toe clip.*
3 *A fore shoe with a feathered edge.*
4 *A hind shoe with studs.*

123

Saddlery

Saddlery is an important aspect of horsemastership. In the interests of safety, appearance, durability and comfort it is important to be able to recognize and buy good quality tack and to look after it correctly.

THE SADDLE

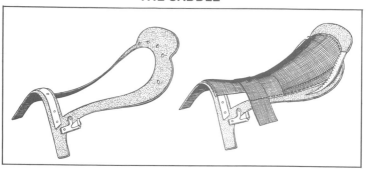

Above: A saddle tree before (left) and after (right) being strained.

The saddle tree

The framework is known as the 'tree', and was traditionally made of beech wood, but laminated wood or metal is more usual today. A 'spring tree' is used in most modern saddles. This has two pieces of tempered steel running lengthwise along the tree from the front arch to the cantle. This makes the seat more resilient and so more comfortable for the rider, who can feel and follow the horse's movements more closely.

The seat

Built on to the tree, this is usually made of pigskin.

The flaps

These are attached to the seat.

The panels

These are stuffed with wool or shaped felt, and act as a cushion between the tree and the horse. There is a channel (gullet) running through the centre, which ensures that weight is not placed on the horse's spine. The panels may be full (reaching almost to the bottom of the saddle flap) or half (reaching only halfway down).

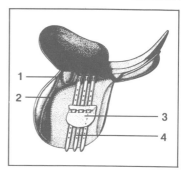

Above: Side view of a saddle.
1 Pocket for point of tree 2 Panel
3 Buckle guard 4 Girth straps.
Below: Underside of a saddle.
1 Cantle 2 Gullet 3 Lining
4 Saddle flap 5 Panel.

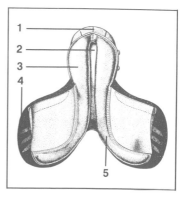

THE SADDLE

The types of saddle
Variation in the design of the tree, panels, etc, are made because the

Parts of a saddle *(Below)*
1. *Pommel*
2. *Skirt*
3. *Twist or waist*
4. *Seat*
5. *Cantle*
6. *Panel*
7. *Girth*
8. *Stirrup leather*
9. *Saddle flap*
10. *'D'*
11. *Skirt*
12. *Stirrup bar closed*
13. *Stirrup leather*

best place for the rider's weight is as near as possible to the centre of gravity of the horse. This varies with changes in the posture and speed of the horse: for example, in racing, the horse is extended and the rider's weight needs to be well forward. In dressage, the horse is collected and the weight needs to be further back.

The jumping saddle
This has to bring the rider's weight well forward. To do this the bars for the stirrup irons are placed forward, the panel is extended and forward cut with rolls to support knee and thigh; the tree is deep.

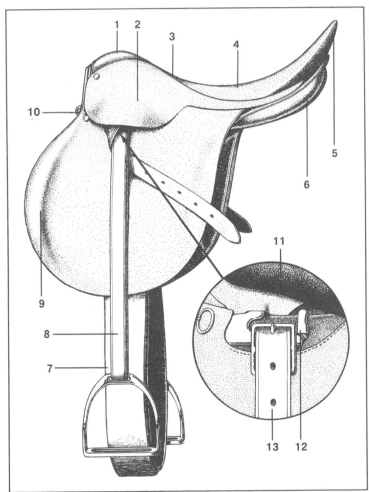

The all-purpose saddle
This saddle is a modification of the above, with panel and flap less forward cut, thus making it possible to ride with longer stirrups.

The dressage saddle
As the rider has to use very long stirrups and to have a deep seat, the dressage saddle is straighter cut, the roll for lower thigh is on the forward edge of the panel, and the dip in the tree is deep, positioning the rider well back.

The show or saddle seat saddle
This is designed to show the front of the horse to its best advantage. It is therefore excessively straight cut and it fits as closely as possible to the horse's back with normally a half panel used, having little padding and no knee rolls.

The racing saddle
The seat is unimportant because the rider rarely sits. Its outstanding feature is that it is very light, weighing about 0.5-1kg (1-2lb). Light materials are used, such as kangaroo-skin and aluminium, the panels are cut to a minimum and the stirrup bars are usually omitted, leathers passing over side bars of the tree.

The stock saddle
This is used for the Western style of riding and has a high pommel with horn in front for securing a lasso when roping. The cantle is also high. Fenders (like long narrow saddle flaps) on each side protect the rider's legs from sweat. There are leather thongs along the back on to which to tie lassos, saddlebags and other gear, and the cinch (girth) is secured by two thongs in cloverleaf knots. The stirrups are wide and of solid wood. Saddle may weigh 13½kg (30lb).

Different types of saddle *(right)*
1 *Jumping saddle*
2 *All purpose saddle*
3 *Dressage saddle*
4 *Showing saddle*
5 *Racing saddle*
6 *Stock saddle*

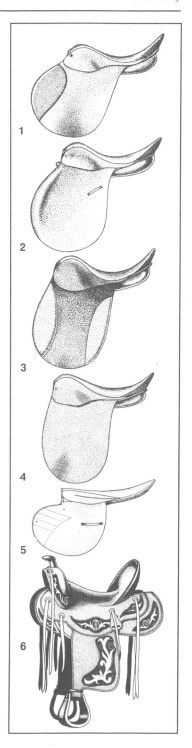

THE SADDLE AND THE BRIDLE

To fit a saddle
An ill-fitting saddle can make both horse and rider sore, and make it difficult for the rider to get into the correct position. It is important to check the saddle carefully, bearing the following points in mind.

The weight must not be concentrated on a particular point but distributed evenly over the back muscles. None must fall on the loin muscles or on the spine. The withers must not be restricted: the front arch of the saddle should be high and wide enough to prevent them from being pinched or pressed upon. The horse's shoulder blades must be able to move freely. Panels must be stuffed so that the rider sits in the correct position. Too much or too little stuffing, or wrong tilting, can result in the rider's seat not being in contact with the horse and/or sliding backwards. It is possible for a tree to break in a fall, or if the saddle itself is dropped. The saddle with a broken tree must not be used, because it would hurt the horse.

To ensure that the saddle fits correctly, it is advisable for the saddler to carry out an annual check-up.

Care of the saddle
When placing the saddle on the ground, rest it on the front arch (not flat), taking care that the leather is not scratched. When carrying, place the front arch in the crook of the elbow. Clean regularly in accordance with general instructions (see below).

Cleaning the lining
Take care to use the appropriate materials. A leather lining should be sponged off, ensuring that water does not run under the lining to dampen the stuffing. Dry with chamois leather, and finally soap. If it is made of linen, sponge or scrub it first, and dry away from direct heat with the saddle standing on its arch. A serge or wool lining should be dried and brushed. It is not advisable to scrub the lining unless it is extremely dirty.

Washing leather
Make sure that the small black spots of grease found under the flap are removed: a small pad of horsehair is the best means of doing this.

The pad or numnah
Worn underneath the saddle, the numnah helps to protect the horse's back. It is made in many types of material, the most common being leather, felt, sponge rubber, synthetic fibres and sheepskin.

It is usually held in place by straps attached to the girth straps. Correctly fitted, it should be large enough to project about 2cm (1in) all round the saddle. Before the girths are tightened, the forward part of the numnah should be pulled up in order not to put pressure on the withers or spine.

Cleaning a numnah depends on the material from which it is made. Leather should be washed with pure soap; felt and sheepskin should be dried and brushed (scrub only when necessary). A synthetic fibre pad may be washed in a machine.

The girth
The girth secures the saddle and there are a number of types.

Web girths
These wear out more quickly than other types and can snap. Always use two.

Leather girths
Excellent as long as they are kept supple and used with caution on soft, unfit horses, when the leather can cause girth galls. They may be shaped, straight, cross-over or three-fold. The last-mentioned should have an oiled flannel inside the fold to keep it soft.

Balding girths
These are narrow in the centre and reduce the chance of rubbing. They allow air to circulate. They are easy to clean with a brush, although an occasional wash is advisable for general cleanliness.

Stirrup irons

The best are made of hand-forged stainless steel. Rubber treads are a useful addition as they help to prevent the rider's foot from slipping. Safety irons are used by many children and these have a rubber band on one side of the stirrup, allowing the foot to come free in a fall. (The rubber is worn on the outside.) This iron does have disadvantages, as it does not hang straight and the rubber often breaks.

A well-fitting stirrup iron should leave the rider's foot with 13mm (½in) on either side, between it and the iron. Less space means the foot might be wedged in a fall, and more can cause the entire foot to slip through.

The bridle

The major purpose of the bridle is to hold the bit in the mouth. The snaffle bridle provides attachments for one bit and the double bridle for two bits.

The snaffle bridle

This, the simpler of the two bridles,

consists of the following:

1 The headpiece and throat latch (lash) are in one piece, with the throat lash preventing the bridle from slipping forwards.
2 The brow band prevents the bridle from slipping backwards.
3 The two cheek pieces are attached at one end to the head-piece and at the other to the bit.
4 The noseband is on its own headpiece.

There are three basic nosebands:

1 The cavesson fastens below the projecting cheekbone and normally serves no purpose other than providing an attachment for the standing martingale.
2 A dropped noseband is fastened under the bit and prevents the horse from evading the bit by opening his mouth.

Parts of the snaffle bridle *(Below)*
1 *Head piece*
2 *Brow band*
3 *Cheek piece*
4 *Cavesson noseband*
5 *Throat latch (lash)*
6 *Snaffle bit*

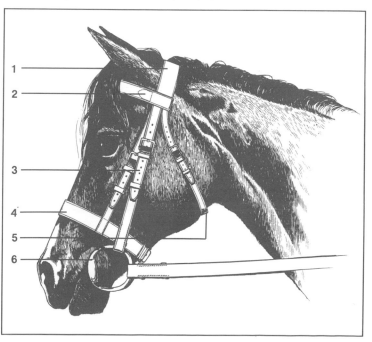

3 The crossed or grackle nose-band has two crossed straps fastening above and below the bit. The pressure preventing the mouth from opening and the jaws from crossing is higher with the grackle than with the dropped noseband.

The bit is attached to the cheek pieces and rein by either stitches (neater), studs (convenient for bit changes) or buckles (convenient, but clumsy in appearance).

The reins have a central buckle. They can be plain, plaited or laced leather (the last two are less likely to slip), covered in a rubber grip (which is the best means of preventing slipping), or plaited or plain linen or nylon.

The double bridle

The double bridle has the same constituents as the snaffle bridle, plus the following:

1 The bridoon headpiece and one cheek piece.
2 Two bits, comprising a bridoon (thin snaffle) and a curb bit (usually called 'the bit').
3 An additional pair of reins of which both are of plain leather, but the bridoon rein is wider than the curb bit rein.
4 The curb chain, which is attached to hooks on either side of the curb bit.
5 The lip strap, which is attached to the small 'D's on the curb bit and runs through the fly link of the curb chain.

To fit the bridle

The throat lash should be loose enough to allow an adult's fist to be placed between it and the jawbone. (If too tight, it restricts the breathing and flexion; if too loose, it will not serve its purpose of preventing the bridle coming over the head, which could lead to a serious accident.)

Different types of bridle [Right]

1 *Bosal bridle*
2 *Western bridle with roping bit*
3 *Cutting horse bit/split ear bridle*
4 *Double bridle*
5 *Hackamore bridle*
6 *Snaffle bridle with drop noseband*

The brow band prevents the bridle from slipping back too far, but must not be so tight that it touches the ears or pulls on the headpiece. The fit of the noseband varies a great deal according to the type.

A cavesson should lie halfway between the projecting cheekbone and the corners of the mouth. Normally, it should be loose enough to

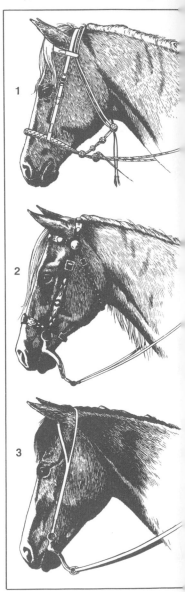

allow two fingers between it and the horse's nose but if done up tightly it can help to prevent the mouth from opening.

A dropped noseband is the normal way of preventing the mouth from opening, but it can be used only with a snaffle bridle and it must be very carefully fitted if it is not to pinch or restrict breathing.

The front piece must be well above the nostrils and the back strap should lie in the chin groove, firmly but not tightly fastened.

The bit must be of the right width and attached so that it hangs in the correct position. If it is too narrow or too high, it will wrinkle or pinch the horse's lips. Too wide or low, it will fall on the teeth. In a double bridle, the bridoon should be higher than the curb bit.

The curb chain is attached to the hook on the offside of the bit, twisted until flat and then attached to the nearside. The length should be such that it comes into play when the bit is drawn back to an angle of 45°.

The lip strap is attached to one side of the curb bit, passed through the fly link of the curb chain and buckled to the other side of the curb bit.

The bit

Bits can be made of various materials. Nickel has a yellow appearance. It is relatively cheap but tends to wear badly, resulting in rough edges, and it may bend or break. Plated steel is stronger than nickel but tends to chip. Hand-forged steel is the strongest but also the most expensive material. Mouthpieces of rubber, rubber-coated metal or vulcanite are comparatively soft, producing a very mild bit.

The purpose of the bit

The bit is used in conjunction with the rider's seat and legs to control the horse. The pressure of the bit on the mouth conveys a message to the horse. With good training, the horse will react by relaxing his jaw and will not resist. He will obey not out of fear or pain but because he has learned to understand and trust his rider. Consequently the key to any horse's mouth does not lie among the numerous types of bits that apply varying degrees of pressure to different parts of the mouth and chin, but in good training, and reliance on a rider with a firm seat and good hands. Mechanical contrivances should

THE BRIDLE AND BIT

be resorted to only if the horse has already been spoilt.

The snaffle

This has a single mouthpiece, which acts upwards against the corners of the lips, particularly when the horse's head is low, on the bars of the lower jaw, particularly when the horse's head is high, and on the tongue. There are many different types and shapes of snaffle.

The snaffle is a very mild bit, especially if made of rubber, and can be used on young, sensitive horses or those with injured mouths.

The single-jointed snaffle has a joint in the centre of the mouthpiece. This creates a 'nutcracker' action causing more pressure to be applied than with the half-moon. It is the most common type of snaffle and has a number of variations.

The thickness of the mouthpiece alters the severity of the bit. The thinner the mouthpiece, the more severe the bit becomes, because the pressure is more concentrated. The thin version is known as a racing snaffle, and the thick one as a German snaffle. The latter is a gentle bit and most riders use it on their young horses.

The rings can be large, small, fixed to the mouthpiece or loose (traversing rings). The two most common types are the egg-butt snaffle (in which the rings are fixed to the mouthpiece and are straight where attached, so that they are less likely to pinch the lips) and the Fulmer snaffle (which has metal cheek pieces to prevent the bit from rubbing the mouth and to ensure the bit is not pulled through from one side to the other). The rings are the loose (traversing) type.

The texture of the mouthpiece also varies. A rough texture helps to prevent the horse or pony from leaning on the bit. The most common variation is the twisted snaffle, in which the mouthpiece is twisted, sharpening the pressure on the horse's mouth. It is a severe

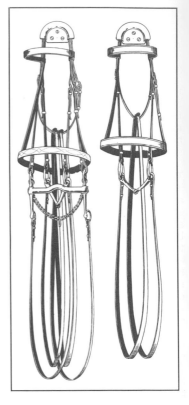

Above: A double bridle (left) and snaffle bridle (right) hung up correctly on wide supports so that the leather keeps its shape and does not crack. The snaffle bridle, the simpler type, is often used with a mild bit on young horses.

bit and should be used only on hard-mouthed horses. Other variations are ridged or square mouthpieces and those with chains and rollers. These are all hard on a mouth and should be used only with caution.

The method of attaching the bit to the leather cheek piece can affect the severity of the bit. The cheek pieces are normally looped on to the rings of the bit, but in the gag-bit they are rounded and pass through holes at the top and bottom of the ring so that the rein is attached directly to the cheek piece. A pull on the rein results in the bit rising against the corners of the horse's mouth. It has a very severe action and the gag-bit should be used only in the last resort.

A double-jointed snaffle has two joints, thus reducing the 'nutcracker' action. Furthermore, the bit will not rest so low and gives the horse more freedom to move his tongue. Sensitive horses and those that put their tongue over the bit are often more relaxed in this snaffle.

The bits of the double bridle

These give a more precise control, and a double bridle, therefore, should not be used until the horse accepts a snaffle bit. To use it before a horse or pony has learned to relax will tend to frighten him, and get him to stiffen against it, so he will obey only because of its severity. The result of this is that he develops resistances in order to try to avoid the action of the bits. The double bridle has two bits.

The bridoon is a snaffle that is usually thinner than the simple snaffle. The curb bit provides additional control and makes possible more refined aids. It acts partly on the tongue, and the pressure is greatest when the mouthpiece is straight. If there is a port in the centre of the curb bit, then there is more room for the tongue to move.

Pressure is also felt on the bars of the mouth (area of gum between the incisor and molar teeth) through the action of the metal cheek piece, which may be fixed (action more direct) or movable; in either case, it has a lever effect.

The third area of pressure is on the curb groove, for as the metal cheek pieces are pulled back, they cause the curb chain to apply pressure on the curb groove. The greater the length of the cheek piece, the greater the leverage and the severity of it and the curb chain.

The fourth area of pressure is on the poll; when the metal cheeks are pulled back, the eye (the ring of the bit to which the leather cheek pieces are attached) goes forward

and, as it is connected to the bridle, exerts down pressure on the poll.

The Pelham

This aims to combine the effect of a snaffle and a curb bit in one. Two reins are normally used. The bridoon rein is attached to rings level with the mouthpiece, and the curb rein to the bottom of the metal cheek piece, thus obtaining the lever and curb chain effect. The mouthpiece may be vulcanite and straight or half-moon, with a port or even jointed.

A 'Pelham converter' or leather roundings are curved couplings that join the bridoon and curb rings on a Pelham bit, so that only one rein need be used. Having only one rein reduces the variation in pressure that can be applied, but it is simpler for the rider to handle.

The Kimblewick

Using the same principle of roundings, it consists of a single, large metal 'D' running from the mouthpiece to the bottom of the cheek piece. It is a severe bit, and must be used with caution.

Parts on which bit works (Below)

1 *Nasal cartilage*
2 *Nasal bone*
3 *Roof of mouth*
4 *Tongue*
5 *Corner of lip*
6 *Bars of mouth*
7 *Chin groove*

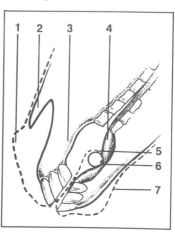

THE BRIDLE AND BIT

The bitless bridle
This bridle has no mouthpiece; pressure is placed on the nose and chin. The hackamore is the best-known type; it has two long metal cheeks that are curved so that their leather attachments act across the nose and behind the chin when the rider pulls on the reins. The same principle is used on a similar type, the bosal bridle.

The principles of bitting
Whenever possible, use the mildest bit. A severe bit can often worry a horse so much that he becomes more excitable and more difficult to control. If the horse resists the bit or is too strong, always consider other possible causes before selecting another bit. These could include bad riding, rough teeth, too much energy-giving food, an injured mouth, a badly fitting bit or bridle, or simply that the horse is too inexperienced to respond.

Different types of bit *(Below)*
1 Egg-butt snaffle
2 Rubber snaffle
3 Double-jointed snaffle
4 Gag-bit
5 Pelham
6 Kimblewick
7 Bridoon & curb bit/double bridle
8 Fulmer snaffle
9 German snaffle
10 Twisted snaffle

If none of these applies, the next step is to analyze the form of resistance before making a selection. If the horse or pony is too strong and has the experience and temperament to accept a stronger bit then try one, but with caution and good hands. If the resistance takes the form of crossing his jaw and opening his mouth, a dropped or crossed noseband should be used. If the tongue is brought over the bit, then the bit is acting only on the bars of the mouth and not on the tongue. To prevent this from occurring make sure the bit is high in the mouth, use a dropped or crossed noseband (as the horse needs to open his mouth to get his tongue over) or try a mouthpiece that has a port or is double-jointed (as these give more freedom for the tongue to lie beneath the bit). If all else fails then a device to prevent the tongue getting over the bit can be used.

The most common forms of resistance are going behind the bit when the head is tucked in, or going above the bit when the head is raised. In the former case a less severe bit is needed, so that the horse will not be frightened to take hold of it. The latter might be due to a lack of training or fear of a severe bit (shown by nervous jerks of the head), and only if the mouth is hard can a curb bit help.

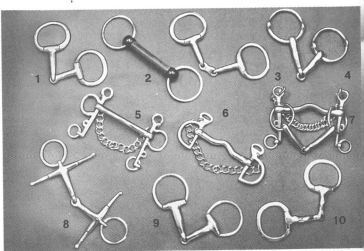

The halter

There are two types of halter, both used to tie up or lead a horse. One is made of hemp or cotton and usually has no throat lash or buckles. The more expensive variety is made of leather or nylon and fitted with buckles and a throat lash. In the USA the term halter still applies, but in the UK this type is known as a headcollar or headstall.

Martingales

These are used to control the position of the horse's head. There are various types.

The standing martingale

This consists of a strap running from the girth to a cavesson noseband (never to a dropped noseband, as this can restrict breathing); it prevents a horse from throwing his head in the air.

The running martingale

This is a strap that runs from the girth, divides in two and ends in rings running along the reins. The effect of this martingale is thus felt on the bit, and a very short running martingale has a severe lever action on the mouth. It should be fitted so that the rings are in line with the withers, thus discouraging the horse from raising his head above this level. The neck strap must not be too tight, as this would rub the animal. Leather or rubber stoppers should be used on the reins to prevent the rings from getting caught on the buckles of the reins.

The Irish martingale

This is used to stop the reins from going over the head.

The Chambon

A strap which runs from the girth through the bit to rings on an attachment over the poll. It is advisable to use the Chambon only on the lunge. It is harmful if used too tightly; ideal only for experts.

The draw rein

This runs from the girth through the rings of the bit to the rider's hands, giving him greater control over the horse's head position. It is frequently used by top show-jumpers but can do much damage in the hands of a rider with limited experience or rough hands.

The breastplate

This is a neck strap with attachments to two 'D's of the saddle and to the girth, which prevents the saddle from slipping back. To fit the breastplate ensure the neck strap is not too tight and that the attachments are not strained.

Below: The draw rein can be seen running from the girth strap.

Putting on the saddle and bridle

Tie up the horse on the halter or headcollar before collecting the saddlery from the tack room. The saddle should be carried with the front arch in the crook of the elbow, with the irons run up, the girth attached on the offside lying over the seat and the pad/numnah (if being used) underneath them all. The bridle and martingale can be hung over the shoulder.

The martingale and the saddle are put on first, so the bridle can be hung up nearby. Check that there is no mud or dirt on the horse where the saddle will lie. Put the neck strap of the martingale over the head so that the buckle is on the nearside.

Putting on the saddle

With the left hand on the front arch and the right hand on the cantle, approach the nearside and place the saddle well forward of the withers. Slide it back so that it sits in the deep part of the back. Check to see that the flaps are straight, and if a numnah is used that it too is flat, pulled well up into the arch of the saddle and protruding evenly around the entire rim of the saddle.

Go to the offside, let down the girth and check that it is straight. Return to the nearside, take the girth, put it through the martingale, if using one, and buckle up. Ensure that the girth is not pinching the skin and that there are enough holes left to be able to tighten it later. Where two webbing girths are used the two should overlap, with the underneath one attached to the forward buckles on either side. Make sure it is done up tightly before mounting.

Above: The boy is carrying the bridle over his left shoulder and the saddle on his lower right arm.
Above right: The saddle with girth on top and stirrups run up is placed well forward of the withers.
Above extreme right: The saddle is then slid back to the low part of the back, the girth slipped over and fastened loosely on near side.
Right: Before tightening the girth, the fingers are run between it and pony to check for wrinkles.
Below: Side and back views show a saddle placed too far forward and resting on the withers. The inset shows the correct position.

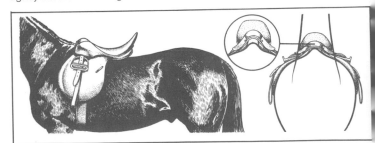

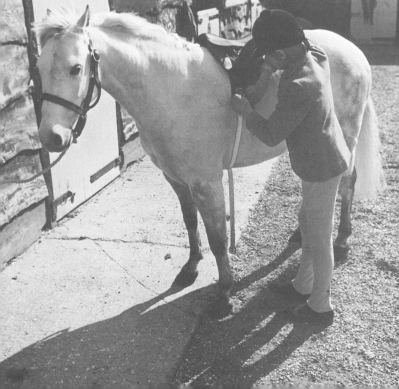

Putting on the bridle

Untie the horse and put the reins over his head. Still holding the bridle, remove the halter and hang it up. With the right hand take the headpiece of the bridle and let the bit rest against the left hand, which is then positioned under the muzzle. Insert the thumb or first finger where there is a gap between the horse's teeth and gently prise the mouth open. The bridle can then be lifted with the right hand while the left hand guides the bit into the horse's mouth. Use both hands to ease the headpiece over the ears, ensuring that no skin or hair is pinched and that the leather is not twisted.

The buckles can then be done up, starting with the throat lash and followed by the noseband, which must lie inside the cheek pieces. All the keepers have to be checked to ensure that the flaps are held in place. With a curb bit, the curb chain must be fastened, twisting it until straight, followed by the lip strap (if there is one).

Check that the bridle is on straight and that the bit is level (ie, that the buckles on both cheek pieces are in matching holes).

With a running martingale the reins should then be undone and put through its rings. With a standing martingale, the loop should be hooked to the noseband before the latter is buckled up.

Right (L to R): Putting on the bridle.
1 With the pony tied up, the bridle is held in the left hand and the reins taken over the head.
2 The halter can be undone and dropped as soon as the reins are securely around the pony's neck.
3 With bit held close, the mouth is opened by pushing the thumb between the molars and the incisors.
4 When the bit goes into the mouth the bridle headpiece is lifted carefully over the ears.
5 The throat latch (lash) is done up first. There should be a fist's space between latch and pony jowl.
6 The noseband buckle is fastened next. The drop noseband shown here must not be too low or tight.

4

THE DRIVING HARNESS

The collar
The collar is a pad that encircles the horse's neck. It can be straight or bent back and is lined with leather, wool or serge, with the outside of brown leather or black patent leather.

It is vital that the collar fits, or the rubbing will cause sores. It should be possible to put the flat of the hand between the top of the collar and the neck; the flat of the fingers at the sides; and the hand and wrist at the bottom.

The breast collar
This serves the same purpose as the collar and is a broad padded strap fitting around the chest and held up by a strap passing over the neck in front of the withers. Although simpler to fit than the collar, it is not considered so smart, nor can such heavy loads be pulled by it.

The hames
These are metal arms that fit around the collar and to which the

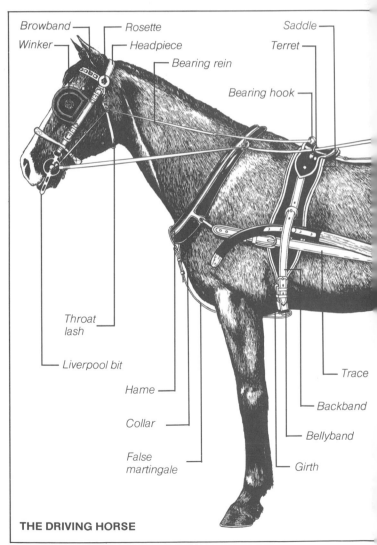

Browband — Rosette — Saddle —
Winker — Headpiece — Terret —
— Bearing rein
— Bearing hook —
Throat lash
— Liverpool bit
Hame —
Collar —
False martingale
— Trace
— Backband
— Bellyband
— Girth

THE DRIVING HORSE

140

traces are attached. The hames must fit into the groove of the collar behind the rim. At the top are driving rings, through which the reins pass. These can be seen clearly in the drawing below.

The hame strap
This fastens the hames at the top and bears a great deal of strain so it must be regularly examined to ensure that it has not stretched or weakened. It is vital to check all parts of the harness regularly.

The driving bridle (*Below*)
1 *Headpiece*
2 *Browband*
3 *Face drop*
4 *Blinker or winker*
5 *Cheek piece*
6 *Noseband*

The army bridle (*Bottom*)
1 *Headpiece*
2 *Browband*
3 *Cheek piece*
4 *Jowl piece*
5 *Bridlehead*
6 *Noseband*

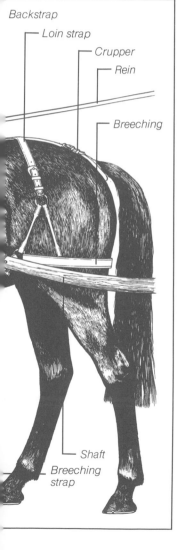

Backstrap
Loin strap
Crupper
Rein
Breeching
Shaft
Breeching strap

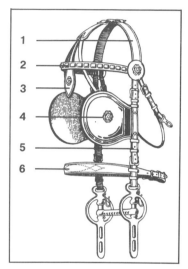

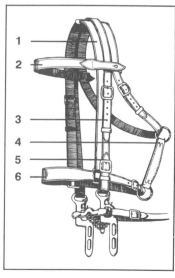

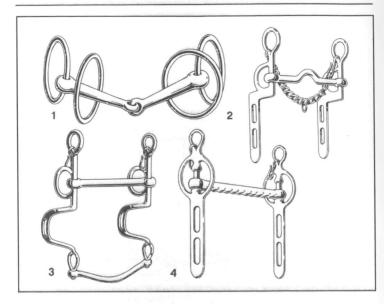

The pad or saddle
The saddle should be used if the horse or pony has to take any of the weight of the vehicle on his back. The pad is a lighter version of the saddle. Like a riding saddle, neither should bear down upon the back and both should be held securely by the girth.

The crupper
The crupper prevents the pad or saddle from slipping forward. It is a back strap connecting the pad or saddle to a crupper dock, which goes under the tail.

The breeching
This enables the horse or pony to stop the vehicle without the assistance of brakes. It hangs horizontally just above the level of the shafts so that when the horse is pulling down hills the strap goes against the animal's quarters, enabling him to hold the vehicle back.

The traces
These connect the collar to the vehicle and bear the strain of pulling the vehicle. They are usually made of leather.

The bridle
There is basically no difference

Types of driving bit (Above)
1 *Wilson snaffle*
2 *Elbow*
3 *Buxton*
4 *Liverpool*

between this and the bridle on a riding horse, but blinkers are usually attached to the cheek pieces. The lower parts of the cheek pieces pass through loops on the inside of the noseband, around the rings of the bit and up to loops on the outside of the noseband, before being buckled.

The bits
These are again basically the same as for riding. The snaffle, however, has two rings on either side. One is fixed on the mouthpiece and the other, which floats along the mouthpiece, is used for the attachment of the bridle's cheek pieces. For more severe action the reins are attached to the floating rings but for gentler control they are buckled to the fixed rings.

The most common curb bits are the Liverpool and the Buxton, the severity of each depending on where the reins are attached to the metal cheeks of the bit; if low down there is a strong leverage but if level with the mouthpiece none.

Regular inspections are essential, because it is safer and cheaper to replace rotting stitches or repair cracked leather in the early stages of deterioration. Tack should always be hung up or stored carefully so that air can circulate around it and prevent mildew. It must be kept clean and the leather in a pliant condition.

Equipment for cleaning tack
In order to clean tack efficiently, the following equipment is needed: a towel for washing; sponge for saddle soap; chamois leather for drying; saddle soap; metal polish and several soft cloths; rubber for drying metal work; dandy brush for removing mud from girths, lining, etc; nail for cleaning out curb hooks, etc; glycerine for covering tack to be stored; a bucket; a hook on which to hang bridles; and a saddle horse.

The dos of tack cleaning
Hang bridle and leather accessories on tack-cleaning hook, and place the saddle on a saddle horse. Undo all buckles and remove fittings (bit, stirrup leathers, irons, etc). Wash leather and metal with lukewarm water and dry with chamois leather. Apply saddle soap to leather with a sponge, using as little water as possible. If using bar soap, it is best to dampen the soap and not the sponge. Apply metal polish to metal and then thoroughly clean off. On any parts of the tack that need washing (eg, girths, pads) use pure soap, not detergent. When cleaning is finished put all the parts together again.

The don'ts of tack cleaning
Never wash leather with washing soda or hot water, or saturate it with water. Never let it dry too close to a strong heat. Never use linseed, neatsfoot oil or mineral oils; use saddle soap, glycerine, olive oil or castor oil to keep leather soft.

Storing the tack
The bridle should be hung up by placing the rein or reins through the throat lash and the noseband outside cheek pieces. There is no need to buckle, but the end of the strap should be put through the keepers. Put the bridle on a wide bridle rack so that the leather keeps its shape and does not crack. Do not use a nail or coat hook. If there is no special hanger, an empty round saddle soap or coffee can, nailed to the wall, makes a good substitute.

The saddle
Place the saddle on a bracket about 45cm (18in) long attached to the wall. The accessories can be hung beside the saddle.

Below: Cleaning tack in a well-equipped and tidy tack room.

Brushing boots
These can be made of many types of material (felt, leather, etc). They are worn around the cannon bone and the upper half of the fetlock joint.

Over-reach boots
These are bell-shaped and fit over the hoof to protect the heels of the forelegs.

Knee caps
Horses' knees can be protected when travelling by the use of knee caps. It is also advisable to use them when exercising on hard roads, in case of a fall.

Hock boots
Worn over the hock, they are made of heavy wool and protect the horse when travelling or, in the stable, if he is a kicker.

Yorkshire boots
These are worn to protect the hind fetlocks and/or coronet.

Above: Protective over-reach boots. Below: A heavy woollen hock boot.

Below: Brushing boots, showing the leather protection pads inside.

Below: Knee caps in place, with travelling bandages also fitted.

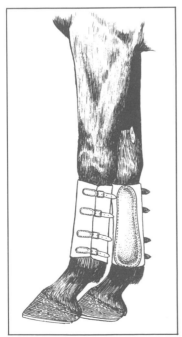

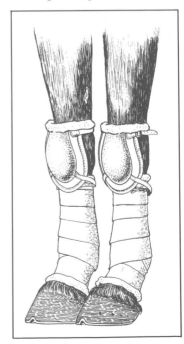

Above: Wrapping a Yorkshire boot around the fetlock before tying.

Below: A Yorkshire boot tied above the fetlock (left); fitted (right).

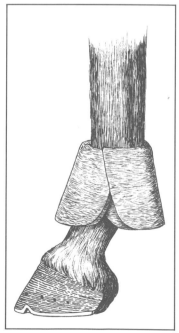

Exercise bandages
Made of stockinette or crepe, 65-75mm (2½-3in) wide, they are used for support and protection. They cover the legs below the knee or hock and above the fetlock joint.

Stable or travelling bandages
These are made of flannel or wool and are about 10cm × 2.5m (4in × 7-8ft). They are used to keep the horse warm, and for protection when travelling. They should cover as much of the leg as possible, from the knee or hock down to the coronet. They should be firmly, but not too tightly, applied over gamgee or cotton wool. Start at the top and wind it around the leg until the fetlock is covered, then work upward until the starting point is reached.

Tail bandage
Made of stockinette or crepe, 6.5-7.5cm (2½-3in) wide, this is used to protect the tail when travelling and/or to improve its appearance by getting the hairs to lie flat. To apply, dampen the tail. Unroll 15cm (6in) of the bandage and hold the end under the tail. Make two turns, to secure the bandage, and then two above, to cover the highest part of the tail; then wind downward around the tail to the end of the tail-bone, where the tapes should be tied. To remove, slide off, grasping bandage at the top of the tail.

To roll up bandages
Tuck tapes in on the side where they are sewn in; then roll up with the sewn side facing inward.

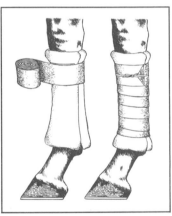

Left: The exercise bandage. This is wound firmly around the leg, starting just below the knee or hock, continuing down to the fetlock joint and then back to the starting point for tying.
Below: The stable or travelling bandage. This is started at the centre of the cannon bone, taken up to below the knee, down to cover the pastern and then back to the knee for tying.
Right: The tail bandage. This is started from the top of the dampened tail and taken down to the end of the tail bone, where it is tied firmly as shown.

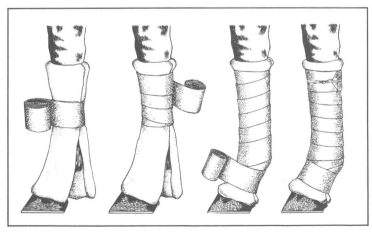

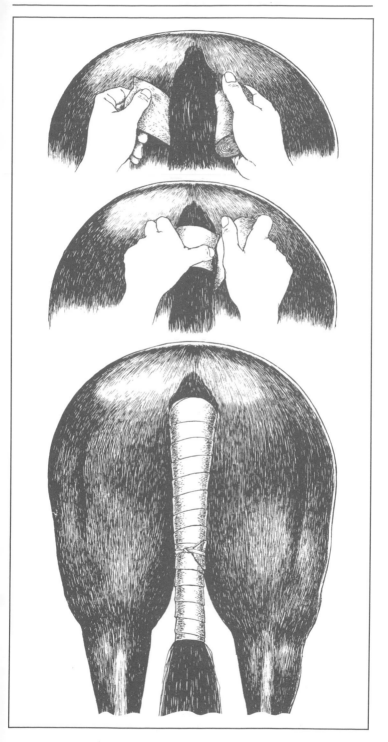

The stable blanket or rug
This is made of heavy jute, hemp or sail canvas and is lined with wool blanketing. It is used in the stable to keep the horse warm.

The day blanket or rug
A wool rug, often decorated with braid, it is used to keep the horse warm when travelling, and on any occasion when he needs to look smart.

The woollen blankets
These are worn under rugs to give extra warmth when it is cold. They are oblong or square.

The roller
This is used to keep rugs in place and is made of leather, web or jute, padded on either side where it passes over the backbone so that presure does not fall on the spine (a pad is often used in addition to give further protection against pressure on the spine). Surcingles, which have no padding, should be used with caution; they often cause sore backs.

The anti-cast roller
Two pads are joined by a metal

Below: A day blanket (rug), used for travelling and for when the horse should look smart.
Bottom: A cooler (sweat sheet). The open mesh of the material allows ventilation for cooling.

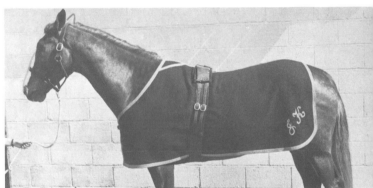

hoop which prevents the horse from rolling over and getting cast.

The summer sheet
Made of cotton, this is used instead of a rug in hot weather. It provides some warmth and is a protection against flies and dust in the summer months.

The cooler or sweat sheet
The holes in this sheet made of open cotton mesh allow ventilation;

Below: A summer sheet, worn when the weather is too hot for a blanket (rug) to be used.
Bottom: A stable blanket (rug) for general use. It provides warmth for the horse in his stall (stable).

it is therefore used for cooling off horses that have sweated. If worn under a rug, it provides a layer of insulation against heat and cold and helps to prevent a horse from 'breaking out' (sweating) after heavy work or other strain.

The New Zealand rug
This is made of waterproof canvas, partly lined with wool, and has special straps to stop it from slipping. It is used to keep horses warm when turned out to grass. For a horse with a full coat, this is unnecessary, but for stabled horses, who may be turned out for a few hours during the day, New Zealand rugs are advisable for extra warmth during cold weather.

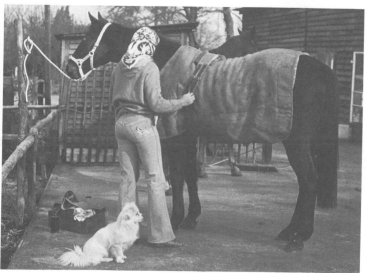

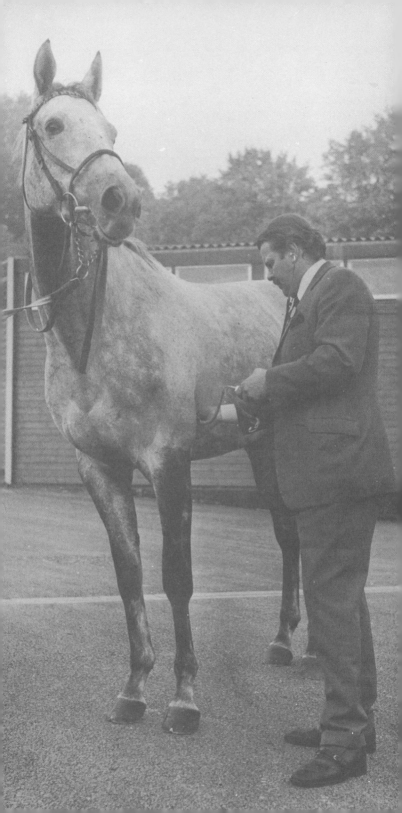

The Health of the Horse

Horses are remarkably tough creatures. In spite of the hazards they have to face—including ignorant owners—the occasions on which they require the attentions of the veterinary profession are usually few. These occasions would be even fewer if horse owners knew the causes of illness and lameness and were careful to avoid them. The advice in this section will help owners to treat simple disorders and to recognize symptoms that require veterinary attention.

THE VETERINARY PROFESSION

Like a doctor, a veterinarian has to undergo a long training; in the UK the course is within a university and takes five years. In addition to the basic sciences the subjects covered are veterinary hygiene and dietetics, pharmacology, bacteriology, pathology, parasitology, medicine and surgery. Those who succeed in their final examinations are awarded a Bachelor of Veterinary Science degree and Membership of the Royal College of Veterinary Surgeons (MRCVS). In the USA the title is Doctor of Veterinary Medicine (DVM), which university graduates can earn after three years.

During veterinary training, there is no special course in equine medicine. Horses are studied as part of the general curriculum and any specialist study must be undertaken as post-graduate work.

Duties of a veterinarian

A very large part of the work entails personal visits to the stables and farms in the area where the veterinarian examines, diagnoses and prescribes treatment for horses.

This veterinary work in the field involves not only treating illness and lameness but also issuing certificates of soundness. These consist of a full description of the animal, the results of a thorough examination, and the final conclusion as to whether in the opinion of the veterinarian the animal is sound or unsound in wind, eye, heart and limb. If requested, the veterinarian will usually also give his opinion as to the suitability of the horse for the proposed work and its chances of remaining sound in the future. In issuing these certificates the veterinarian plays a major part in the buying and selling of horses, and in their insurance (a company will not insure an animal without such a certificate).

Veterinarians are also trained as surgeons, and in this field there have been great advances due to improvements in anaesthesia. Major operations are usually performed in special operating theatres. Minor operations, though, can still be performed at the patient's stable.

X-rays play a large part in equine diagnosis and, although there are some mobile units that can be brought to the stables, the best results are gained from bringing patients to a practice where there is a permanent machine.

Professional etiquette

Veterinarians are governed by rules of professional conduct, and owners are most affected by the one forbidding a veterinarian to take over a case from another veterinarian without agreement. If a horse owner is dissatisfied with the treatment his animal is receiving, he should inform the veterinarian that he no longer wishes him to attend the case, ask for him to bring a 'second opinion', or if it is a serious case request a consultant specialist in the particular field. If an owner fails to follow this procedure, he may find it difficult in the future to get the co-operation of a veterinarian.

ANATOMY OF THE HORSE

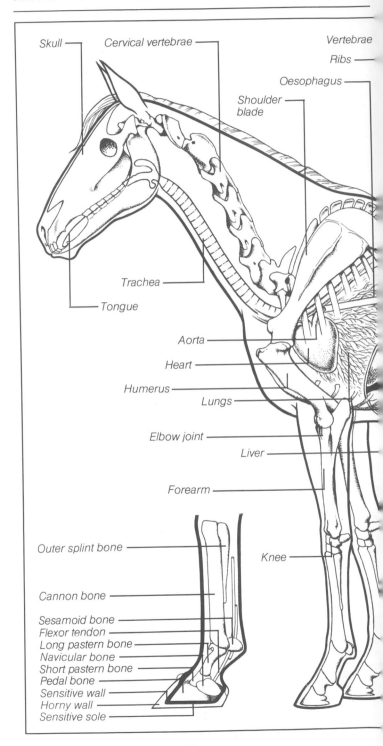

Skull

Cervical vertebrae

Vertebrae

Ribs

Oesophagus

Shoulder blade

Trachea

Tongue

Aorta

Heart

Humerus

Lungs

Elbow joint

Liver

Forearm

Outer splint bone

Knee

Cannon bone

Sesamoid bone
Flexor tendon
Long pastern bone
Navicular bone
Short pastern bone
Pedal bone
Sensitive wall
Horny wall
Sensitive sole

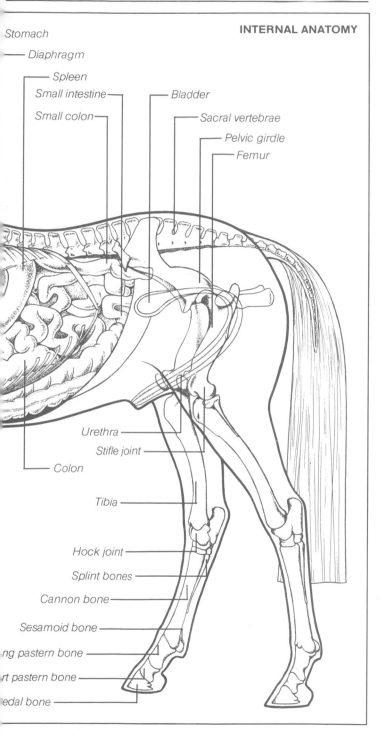

INTERNAL ANATOMY

Stomach

Diaphragm

Spleen

Small intestine

Small colon

Bladder

Sacral vertebrae

Pelvic girdle

Femur

Urethra

Stifle joint

Colon

Tibia

Hock joint

Splint bones

Cannon bone

Sesamoid bone

ng pastern bone

rt pastern bone

edal bone

1 Lacks interest in feed, loses weight, becomes 'tucked up' (hind part of abdomen gets smaller).
2 Droppings— no longer round balls that break on hitting the ground; bad smell; shape and/or consistency changes; mucus or parasites visible in them; may not be passed regularly.
3 Coat becomes dull and/or tight. Horse starts sweating.
4 Eyes become dull and unalert.
5 Discharge from the eyes and the nostrils.
6 Legs become puffy.
7 Temperature above or below the normal 37.7-38.3°C (100-101°F). Temperature should be taken with clinical thermometer that has been lubricated with oil or soap. The tail is raised and the

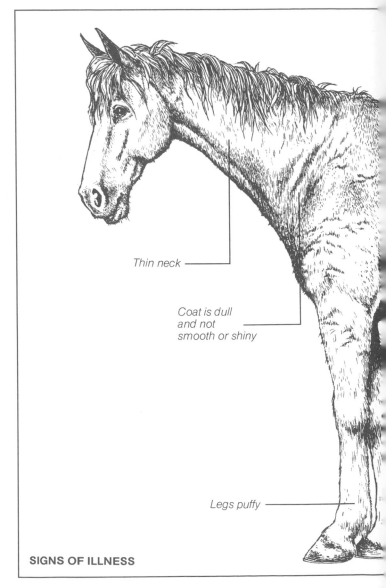

Thin neck

Coat is dull and not smooth or shiny

Legs puffy

SIGNS OF ILLNESS

thermometer inserted into the rectum. Thermometer must touch one side and not stay in the middle, where it would measure only the temperature of the faeces.

8 Breathing looks restricted and respiratory rate rises (normal rate is 10-15 a minute; can be counted by watching flank rise and fall).

Any of these signs of illness should lead to a careful examination to ascertain whether a simple explanation (eg, sweats due to hot weather) can be found. If not, and especially if condition is deteriorating, a veterinarian should be called. It is helpful to the veterinarian if careful note of all signs of illness has been taken and an account of the horse's recent activities made.

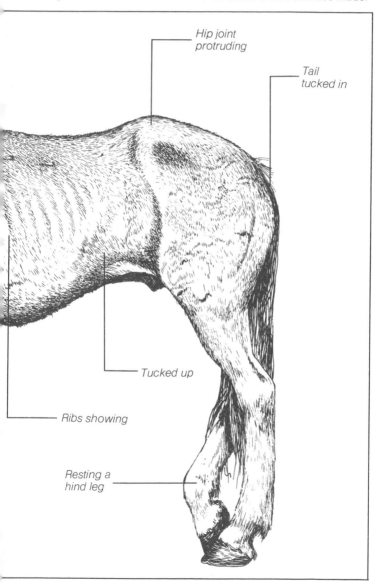

Hip joint protruding

Tail tucked in

Tucked up

Ribs showing

Resting a hind leg

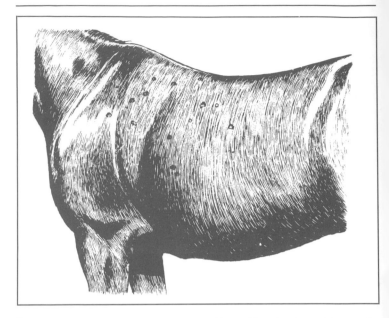

Ringworm

Circular patches caused by fungus.

Symptoms: Small, round, hairless patches develop, exposing greyish, scaly skin. The horse tends to lose condition.

Treatment: Paint iodine on to every single patch daily. It is essential that not one is missed and it is often a help to clip the horse. Ringworm is exceptionally contagious, so the victim should be isolated. Tack and groom kit should be kept separate. Attendant should change clothes before approaching another horse. Any item that comes into contact with the victim should be disinfected. (Humans can be infected by some forms of ringworm.)

A veterinarian should usually be consulted; he can often recommend a more effective form of treatment than the traditional iodine.

Prevention: This fungus is best prevented by thorough disinfecting of any strange tack, stable/stall or transportation, especially if there is a possibility that a horse with ringworm might have used them.

Above: The circular patches on the skin typical of ringworm infection.

Lice

Lice-infested skin.

Symptoms: Itchiness; small patches, which the horse tries to rub. Careful examination reveals slate-grey lice, up to 1.5mm (1/16in) long, or nits (eggs) on the skin.

Treatment: It is advisable to clip the horse, then apply lice-powder or -wash; repeat every few days. The horse is likely to lose condition, so he must be fed well and given mineral additives.

Prevention: Cleanliness of horse and stable.

Sweet itch

An irritation of the skin, usually confined to the crest, withers and croup. It tends to occur annually in the late spring and summer.

Symptoms: Horse rubs affected areas, eventually removing the hair and exposing a wrinkled inflamed skin.

Treatment: Sunshine appears to agitate irritation, so keep horse stabled by day. Lotions (zinc and sulphur ointment, sulphur and tar, or calamine) applied to the area usually ease the irritation.

Nettlerash
Round swellings on the skin's surface.
Symptoms: Squeezy bumps that do not cause irritation.
Treatment: Laxative diet. Administration of anti-histamine.
Prevention: Attention to diet; avoid sudden changes in types of food. Too much high-energy food (especially accompanied by too little exercise) and lush spring grass can bring on nettlerash.

Mud fever
An inflammation of the skin occurring on the inside of limbs and/or on the belly.
Symptoms: Puffiness and heat in legs. Skin gets rough, scabby and sore. Occasionally horse becomes lame.
Treatment: Essential to keep legs dry. If they get muddy, dry and brush off; or, if necessary to wash, dry thoroughly with chamois leather or dry cloth.
     Apply soothing lotion or cream (zinc ointment, lanolin — or other treatment, prescribed by veterinarian).
Prevention: Avoiding riding in the muds that are known to cause it. After work, ensure legs are thoroughly dry and avoid excessive washing. Horses with

white hair on legs tend to be more liable, so special care must be taken with them.

Warbles
Warble-fly maggots hatch from eggs laid on the horse. The maggots get into the horse's system and appear as small lumps under the skin.
Symptoms: Small lumps, usually in the saddle region.
Treatment: Attempts to remove maggot might cause an infection. If left, the maggot bores its way out of the skin, after which iodine or antibiotic powder should be applied to the hole. A saddle should not be placed on top of a bump containing the warble maggot, as it will cause soreness.

Cracked heels
Cracks in the hollow at the back of the pastern.
Symptoms: Skin becomes sore, red and scabby.
Treatment: As for mud fever.
Prevention: As for mud fever. Horses that tend to develop cracked heels can have their heels coated with petroleum jelly or lanolin before work.

Below: Clear signs of cracked heels at the back of the pasterns.

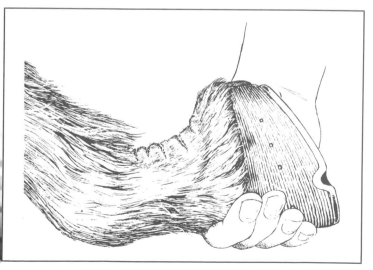

RESPIRATORY AILMENTS

Colds
Symptoms: Thin nasal discharge, becoming thicker.

Treatment: Isolate, keep warm, consult a veterinarian, who may decide to administer antibiotics if the cold is severe.

Prevention: As for humans: avoid subjection to extremes of temperature.

Coughs
Treatment: This varies according to cause of cough. A horse brought up from grass may develop a cough, so try to keep conditions as constant as possible (food, temperature, etc). If a sore throat or laryngitis causes cough, keep horse warm and give small doses of a good cough syrup on tongue and back of teeth, two or three times a day.

If poor condition might be cause of cough, it is wise to test for worms. In all cases, dampen food, put on laxative diet and do not over-exert. Exercise is advisable only if the cough is very mild; even then, no hard work must be undertaken.

Broken wind
Respiratory distress due to the breakdown of air vesicles or vessels (alveolar walls) of the lung.

Symptoms: A deep, persistent cough. Expiratory movements of chest are exaggerated and horse's flank can be clearly seen to heave twice during each exhalation.

Treatment: Incurable unless caused by an allergy but effects can be alleviated by avoiding dust and an excess of bulk food. Linseed oil about three times a week is a help; food should be dampened and stable bedding should be of shavings or peat so that horse cannot eat straw or inhale dust.

Prevention: Do not give dusty food, especially prior to work. Care must be taken with sufferers of a respiratory complaint; asking a horse to work with a cough can lead to broken wind.

Whistling
Caused by rupture of one of the nerves of the larynx resulting in paralysis of the vocal cord. Whistlers make a high-pitched noise when breathing in.

Symptoms: Whistling rarely heard until the horse is asked to work. More pronounced at the faster paces.

Treatment: *Tubing:* The veterinarian inserts into the windpipe a tube though which the horse can breathe freely.

Hobdaying: An operation to remove the membrane from the pouch behind the vocal cord. In a successful operation, the cord sticks to the wall of the larynx so that there is no obstruction to the progress of wind through the passage.

Prevention: Can be hereditary; occurs only in larger horses.

Roaring
Due to partial paralysis of the soft palate.

Symptoms: Horse makes a deep, rumbling noise during exhalation at exercise.

Treatment: Difficult to treat. Line firing of the soft palate has been recommended.

Prevention: Avoid working too soon after an attack of strangles.

High-blowing
An abnormality of the false nostril resulting in noisy exhalation. High-blowing is not an unsoundness and does not restrict breathing.

Influenza
Contagious virus infection.

Symptoms: These vary according to the strain of the virus; usually temperature rises, horse goes off his food, becomes lethargic and often starts to cough.

Treatment: Isolation. Warmth, tempting food, and the attention of a veterinarian. Rest; any exertion can lead to pneumonia and permanent damage to the respiratory passages if the cough has not gone.

Prevention: Immunize with injections, followed by an annual

booster. In the case of an outbreak, take the temperature of all horses before work (a rise in temperature is normally the first indication of influenza).

Strangles

A disease affecting the lymph glands, usually only those of horses under six years old are affected.

Symptoms: Lethargy, temperature rises as high as 40°C (105°F), nasal discharge, glands under jaw swell and eventually form an abscess, which usually bursts.

Treatment: As the disease is highly contagious, isolate horse and disinfect all items that come in contact with the victim. Convalescence must be taken slowly. The disease lasts about six weeks; this period must be followed by two or three months of gentle work or some time in the field.

Below: Swollen lymph glands under the jaw may indicate strangles.

NON-RESPIRATORY
Azoturia

Usually occurs after hard exercise that has been preceded by a period of rest during which the horse remained on full rations.

Symptoms: Stiffness of the muscles of the loins and quarters may cause staggering; eventually, the horse can collapse. The horse sweats, his breathing speeds up and his temperature rises. If any urine is passed, it is brownish.

Treatment: If azoturia starts when riding, dismount and allow horse to rest. Arrange for his transportation back to stables so he does not have to walk. Keep warm, massage tight muscles, give plenty of water and feed a laxative diet. Call a veterinarian.

Prevention: Always reduce diet when horse is to be rested (hence tradition of giving a mash on Saturday night, Sunday being a rest day). Azoturia is likely to recur; diet must, therefore, always be adjusted according to work, and plenty of exercise should be given daily, by riding or turning out to grass.

Tetanus (lockjaw)

An infection caused by bacteria that live in the soil and penetrate the horse's skin through an open wound. Tetanus is fatal unless treated quickly.

Symptoms: Symptoms are never noticed until well after the bacteria have entered through the wound. The horse starts to move stiffly and the third eyelid flickers across the eye. Co-ordination becomes increasingly restricted. Jaws eventually lock.

Treatment: The veterinarian must be called, to give doses of serum. Stable must be kept darkened and absolutely quiet; diet should be laxative and plenty of water should be available.

Prevention: Two injections followed by an annual booster, then 3- to 5-yearly boosters, provides immunity from this dreadful disease.

If any horse that has not undergone this permanent immunization is wounded (particularly a puncture wound), or if there is any doubt as to whether such a horse has been immunized, then a veterinarian should be called to give an injection of anti-tetanus serum.

DIGESTIVE PROBLEMS

Sharp teeth

If upper jaw grows down and outward while lower jaw groups up and inward, uneven wear of teeth and formation of sharp edges that cut tongue and cheeks can result.

Symptoms: Chewing becomes painful so horse may not masticate food (whole oats seen in droppings) and/or not eat up and so lose condition. Sharp teeth can be felt if mouth is opened, the tongue held and finger run over teeth.

Treatment: Floating (rasping) teeth by a veterinarian or specialist.

Prevention: Regular inspection and floating (rasping) of teeth.

Colic

Abdominal pain; equine 'tummy ache'.

Symptoms: *Spasmodic colic* pain fluctuates; horse may be free from pain for up to an hour before next attack. When in spasm, horse appears unsettled, paws ground, lies down and gets up, tries to roll, may look at belly and start to sweat. Temperature may rise and breathing become hurried.

Flatulent colic, or wind colic, is due to partial or temporary obstruction in the bowels, leading to a build-up of gas. Pain tends to be continuous and not so severe. The horse rarely tries to lie down but otherwise symptoms are the same as for spasmodic colic.

Twisted gut occurs when the membrane suspending the bowel becomes twisted or when the bowel becomes twisted on itself, so cutting off the blood supply. The pain is more severe and the temperature higher.

Treatment: As long as the horse is not exhausted, it is best to lead him for quiet walks. He should be kept warm, the stable well bedded and he should be constantly watched to ensure no injury occurs if he should get down and roll. For wind colic, give a laxative; 0.25-0.51 (½-1pt) linseed oil depending on the size. For spasms give a colic drink, which you should have from the veterinarian and keep with the first-aid equipment. If no improvement occurs after an hour, or if pain is severe, call for professional help, and you should stay with the horse until the veterinarian arrives.

Constipation

Symptoms: Droppings not passed regularly and consistency becomes hard.

Treatment: Bran mashes, green food, 0.25-0.51 (½ to 1pt) linseed oil or 14-85g (½-3oz) Epsom salts in water or food.

Worms

Intestinal parasites found in all horses; when present in large numbers worms may cause severe problems.

The most common types are:

Small strongyles, which do not usually cause problems unless another infection impairs the horse's overall health.

Large strongyles (red worms), reddish in colour and up to 5cm (2in) long, which spend their adult life in the bowel; earlier in their life cycle they pass through the abdomen, where they often damage blood vessels. Because they suck blood, they can cause anaemia. These are sometimes called blood worms. The eggs are passed out in the faeces.

Symptoms: Horse loses condition, bowel movement tends to be irregular. Eggs are passed out in the droppings; a fresh dung sample can be examined under the microscope for a worm egg count.

Treatment: The veterinarian will recommend the best remedy.

Large roundworms (ascarids), white or yellow and up to 7mm (¼in) in diameter and 30cm (12in) in length. They are a problem only with young horses.

Treatment: The veterinarian can dose through a stomach tube

Whipworms, thin parasites about 25-45mm (1-1¾in) long that live in the rectum. The female lays eggs around the anal region, where they can be seen as a waxy mass. They cause irritation so horse rubs tail.

Treatment: The veterinarian will recommend the best modern dosage.

Prevention: Regular doses of a wormer is the best method. Precautions must be taken against paddocks becoming 'horse sick': ie having grass on which there are many worm larvae. (Worm eggs pass out in droppings, and hatch out; hatched larvae attach themselves to grass stems; horses that eat the grass become infected.)

This state is prevented by: regular worming, which will reduce the production of worm eggs; changing the stock on particular fields on an annual basis (horse worms will not generally infect sheep and cattle, and vice versa); removing droppings from the pasture; reducing overall horse-stocking density; ploughing and re-seeding.

Diarrhoea

Symptoms: Droppings loose.

Treatment: Kaolin can be given with food, but best to ask for veterinary medicine. Feed hay and not fresh grass.

Prevention: Spring grass is a common cause, and hay should therefore be substituted as soon as possible.

WOUNDS AND INJURIES

Treatment of wounds: If bleeding does not stop of its own accord, apply a pressure bandage over wound. Call the veterinarian immediately, if stitching is required. Clean wound; clip away surrounding hair if it is in the way. Trickle cold water from a hose pipe over wound, or use salt and water. If the wound is a puncture, leave any probing to the veterinarian. Harsh antiseptics and disinfectants are no longer recommended as they kill healing cells as well as harmful organisms. Dress the wound with antibiotic powder. Protect, if necessary and possible,

by applying a bandage lightly over a layer of cotton wool, with lint next to the wound. Give anti-tetanus injection, if not already immunized. Ensure maximum cleanliness of surroundings. If swelling is excessive, use fomentations.

Antibiotics are advisable for punctures, especially if wound is near joint, tendon sheath or foot.

Constant attention to potential signs of infection: refusing food, extension of swelling, sweating.

Mouth injuries

Use salt-and-water washes. Avoid use of bit until healed. Change bit, if injury was due to it.

Girth gall

Occurs on soft skin behind the elbow, due to the girth's rubbing. Treat injury with fomentations; when healed, use salt and water or methylated spirit to harden. Avoid using saddle for a few days and then use a more comfortable girth.

Saddle-soreness

Due to the saddle's rubbing, so do not ride in a saddle until soreness heals. Ensure cause of problem (eg badly fitting saddle) is removed. Use a thick numnah with a hole cut over the sore. Treat as for girth galls.

Broken or cut knees

Usually caused by a fall on to knees. If injury is more than skin deep, call a veterinarian. Otherwise, treat with slow trickle of cold water from a hose pipe. Apply kaolin poultice but no bandage.

Capped knee

A swelling resulting from a blow to the knee. Treat with rest, massage, pressure bandage and, if swelling persists, a mild blister.

Capped hock

A swelling around the point of the hock, due to a blow or kick.

Treatment: Prevent aggravation of injury by providing thick bedding and the use of hock boots when travelling. Cold treatment followed by a poultice. If swelling persists, apply a mild blister.

If lameness renders a horse unfit to work, he must be fed a laxative diet.

Finding the seat or place of the lameness

1 Decide which leg is causing the pain by watching horse being led at the trot (it shows best if trotted downhill).
2 Search with eyes and hands for heat, pain and swellilng. Start with the feet, as they are the most common source of lameness.
3 Call in a veterinarian, if there is danger of infection or any doubt as to reason for lameness.

Pricks and punctures

Symptoms: Localized tenderness, heat swelling of pastern.
Treatment: Remove nail or other cause of puncture/prick. Scrape hole to release pus. Poultice, or submerge foot in bucket of warm salty water for 20 minutes several times a day and clean out hole. After a few days, apply liquid antiseptic to a puncture. Rest patient until sound. Call the veterinarian if in doubt.
Prevention: Errors when shoeing are a common cause, so care should be taken to choose a blacksmith of good repute.

Corns

Bruises to the sole in heel region.

Below: Corns can develop on the sole either side of the frog.

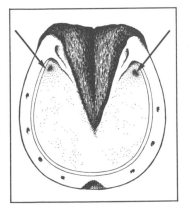

Symptoms: Lameness increases with work. Sensitivity to sharp blows over heels. To confirm, professional must remove shoe and pare horn away, to search for corn (red spot).
Treatment: Remove shoe. Poultice, if severe. Re-shoe with ¾-length shoes. Rest.
Prevention: Avoid pressure on seat of corn by: (a) careful shoeing, (b) frequent shoeing, to prevent hooves growing long.

Founder (laminitis)

'Fever in the feet', due to inflammation of the sensitive tissue lining the inside wall of the foot.
Symptoms: Acute pain shown by reluctance to move; flinching observed when sole of affected foot tapped. Horse stands with weight on heels. In chronic cases of laminitis, ridges (due to horn being produced irregularly) form on the hoof.
Treatment: Relieve inflammation and pain. Ask the veterinarian to give an injection of cortisone or anti-histamine. Give cold treatment (stand horse in, or hose feet with, cold water). Remove his shoes, get feet cut down and exercise him on soft going.
Prevention: Avoid feeding too much, especially rich food (barley, wheat, etc), and take care when he is first put out on

Below: A laminitic foot, with ridges developing on the hoof.

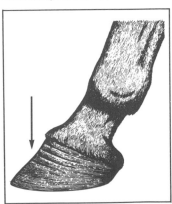

spring grass. Frequent and regular exercise. Do not go at a fast trot on hard roads. Take special care of horses with flat feet and weak horn. If disease is diagnosed, prompt treatment is essential to prevent a permanent disability due to a change in structure of the foot.

Pedal Ostitis
Bruising of the pedal bone (usually in forelegs).

Symptoms: 'Going short' (trotting with short strides). Heat in foot. Lameness, wearing off with exercise. X-ray to confirm.

Treatment: Turn out to grass where land is soft, for six or more months. Introduction to work should be gradual and start with walking.

Prevention: Avoid riding horse hard on firm or stony ground.

Bruised sole
Symptoms: Sole tender under pressure.

Treatment: Rest.

Prevention: Thin-soled horses are especially susceptible; they are less vulnerable if shod with a leather sole or pads.

Canker
A disease of the horn; tissue is secreted in and spreads from the frog.

Symptoms: Grey-white discharge; spongy swellings on frog. Pain is not severe.

Treatment: As for thrush, but canker is more serious. It calls for immediate treatment and the attention of the veterinarian.

Prevention: As the cause has not been confirmed, there is no specific preventative measure, but cleanliness helps.

Thrush
A disease of the cleft of the foot, in which the glands of the region excrete excessively.

Symptoms: Nasty odour from discharge.

Treatment: With brush, soap and water, clean frog and cleft. If severe, apply poultice; if mild, apply boracic powder, sulphanilamide or Stockholm tar to dried cleft. Shoe so that heels are lowered, bringing frog into contact with the ground. Keep in gentle exercise, unless lameness is severe.

Prevention: Attention to cleanliness. Feet must be picked out regularly and bedding not allowed to get dirty or damp. Care that horse is shod so that frog touches the ground and is thus able to function.

Sandcrack
Symptoms: The wall of the hoof cracks and splits.

Treatment: Grooves can be burned into wall with a hot iron, to cross the crack at the top and bottom. Encourage new horn to grow with applications of a mild blister to coronet band or of cornucrescine to hoof, and good food. Crack can be stopped from opening by professional insertion of a nail across the crack and clenching at both ends.

Prevention: Weak, brittle feet especially liable. Regular applications of cornucrescine and attention to diet encourage a better growth of horn.

Navicular disease
The navicular bone changes in shape and texture, making it

Below: An example of a severe sand crack in the wall of the hoof.

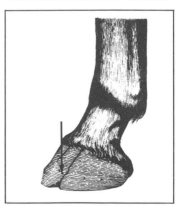

painful for the flexor tendon to run over the surface. It is suspected that the disease is hereditary and may be induced by trotting fast on roads.

Symptoms: Initially intermittent lameness. Usually points the affected foot in the stable. X-ray needed to confirm diagnosis.

Treatment: No satisfactory treatment has yet been discovered. With early diagnosis, steps can be taken to relieve the pressure of the tendon's passing over the navicular bone. Shoes with thin rolled toes and thick heels will help in this.

Neurectomy/denerving is the only means of keeping developed cases in work. In this operation, the affected sensory nerves are cut so that the horse will not feel the pain.

Splint

Bony enlargement of splint bones or cannon bone, or between any of these three bones. Usually found on inside of forelegs.

Symptoms: Pressure from fingers on area results in the horse's flinching. Splint can usually be seen.

Treatment: It is usually only during the formation of the splint that pain occurs, unless near the knee joint or by the suspensory ligament. Normally, six weeks is enough time for recovery but if lameness persists, the splint can be blistered or pin-fired. During time of pain, cold treatment, a working blister or an injection of cortisone can help to speed recovery. The horse should only be walked.

Prevention: Splints can be caused by blows; brushing boots or bandages worn during work reduce this risk. Excessive work on immature legs should be avoided. NB Splints are rarely thrown by horses over six years.

Bone spavin

Enlargement of the bone on the lower and inner side of the hock.

Symptoms: Lameness usually wears off with exercise. The hock moves stiffly, which usually results in the hind toe being dragged.

Treatment: A long rest is advisable. Hot fomentations, alternated with cold-water treatment, helps to reduce the initial inflammation. Blistering or pin-firing can be of use; but surgical treatment may be necessary.

Prevention: Bone spavin is thought to be hereditary, but excessive work or exertion, especially with young horses, may bring it on. Horses with cow, sickle or weak hocks tend to be more vulnerable to spavins because of the abnormal stress.

Bog spavin

Fluid distension of the hock joint capsule; shows as a soft swelling on the front inner side of the hock.

Symptoms: Bulges can be seen. Heat is rarely present, except in

Signs of a splint (*Below*)
1 *Splint on inside of off foreleg*
2 *Splint bones*
3 *Splints*
4 *Cannon bone*

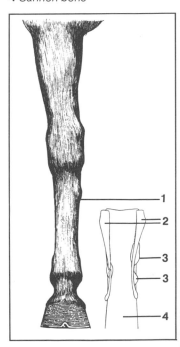

acute cases. Lameness occurs only if swelling interferes with action.

Treatment: None necessary for horse that is not lame. If needed, cold treatment, astringents and massage help. Rest and pressure bandaging may be necessary. Firing is advisable for bad cases, or injections into the area of the sprain.

Prevention: Where there are signs of a bog spavin, shoeing with high heels and rolled toes helps to relieve the strain. As in the case of the bone spavin, horses with straight, cow or sickle hocks are more vulnerable and should not be subjected to excessive work or exertion, especially when young.

Thoroughpin

A small swelling above and in front of the point of the hock.

Symptoms: Rarely leads to lameness, except if caused by recent injury. The swelling can be seen;

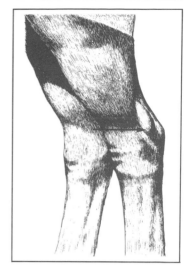

Above: A thoroughpin on the hock.

larger ones go through from one side of the hock to the other.

Treatment: Thoroughpins are no problem unless very large, when

Below: A bone spavin on the inner side of the near hock.

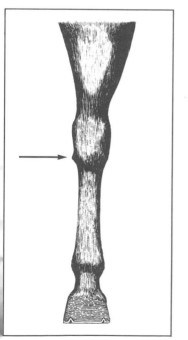

Below: A bog spavin on the inner side of the near hock.

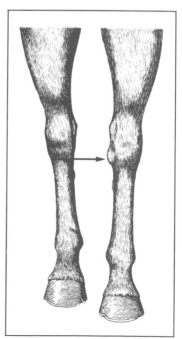

the horse should be rested and blistered, or the vet can give an injection of hydrocortisone. In normal cases, massage helps to get rid of them.

Prevention: Avoidance of exercise that might put an exceptional strain on the hocks, especially in the case of a young horse or one with weak hocks.

Curb

Enlargement, visible below the point of the hock, due to enlargement of the ligament that attaches the bones of the hock to the cannon bone.

Symptoms: The enlargement can be seen when looking at the hock from the side. Lameness is rare.

Treatment: If causing lameness, inflammation should be removed with kaolin poultice or cold-water treatment. The horse should rest.

Prevention: Excessive strain should not be inflicted on the hocks of young horses, especially those with weak hocks, by too much galloping and jumping. When early signs of a curb appear, the horse should be given a period of rest.

Sprained tendon

Symptoms: Heat and swelling always present. In bad cases, there is a bow when leg looked at from the side (in the UK referred to as 'broken down'). As foot problems often cause swelling to rise up the tendon, it is wise to remove shoe and ensure that lameness does not come from the foot, before attempting to treat the tendon.

Treatment: Rest is most important. If swelling is slight, use cold treatment. If more severe, alternate hot poultice (animalintex, antiphlogistine or kaolin) with cold treatment. It may be advisable to follow this with blistering or firing and a long rest. The re-introduction to work should be graduated, starting with long walks on the roads to toughen up the tendons without jarring or straining. Call a veterinarian for severe cases.

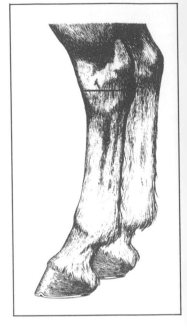

Above: A curb below the hock.

Sprained fetlock joint

Symptoms: Heat and swelling around the joint.

Treatment: Rest. Kaolin poultice, which can also be alternated with cold treatment. As for

Below: Wind galls, small swellings that appear above the fetlocks.

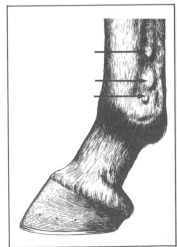

sprained tendons; the re-introduction to work must be gradual.
Prevention: Horses with upright joints, which are not so elastic, are more liable to this injury and care must be taken to avoid jarring them on hard ground or twisting legs in rough going.

Wind galls
Usually small swellings found above the fetlocks, arising from strain in the fetlock joint itself, which causes excess joint fluid to be secreted.
Symptoms: The swelling can be seen and felt.
Treatment: Can be reduced with cold treatment or by using pressure bandages when at rest.
Prevention: Avoid strain, toes growing long and heels too low.

Ring-bone
Bony enlargement of the pastern bone. A 'low' ring-bone is in the coronet region, a 'high' above the coronet.
Symptoms: Lameness usually occurs only if enlargement interferes with the movement of the pastern joint. Tendency for heat and pain to develop on hard ground. Eventually 'high' ring-bone can be felt but a 'low' ring-

Below: A 'low' ring-bone (left) and a 'high' ring-bone (right).

bone is more difficult and usually needs an X-ray for accurate detection.
Treatment: Rest. Cold treatment can be used to reduce inflammation. Cortisone can be injected. If lameness persists, blistering or pin-firing may be necessary.
Prevention: Care should be taken lest feet grow too long, which would prevent the frog from doing its work of absorbing jar. Horses with upright or very long pasterns are more susceptible; care should be taken not to work them on hard ground. Sharp blows and pulled ligaments will induce a ring-bone, so a clumsy horse should undergo corrective shoeing. It is thought to be hereditary in some cases.

Side-bone
Ossification of the lateral cartilages of the foot.
Symptoms: Can be felt. Lameness unusual, unless foot starts to contract leading to pressure on sensitive areas.
Treatment: No need for any unless horse starts to go lame; then rest and apply cold treatment. Blacksmith can shoe so as to encourage expansion of hoof. Blistering or firing can be used.
Prevention: Side-bone is thought to be hereditary; but concussion or a blow may bring it on.

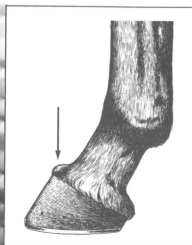
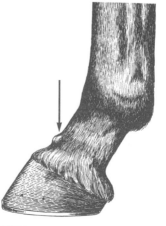

Biting

Causes: Ticklishness. Bad treatment. The giving of snacks. Playful nibbling not corrected.

Remedies:

1 Handle kindly but firmly; reprimand with voice or slap on muzzle.
2 Take care not to irritate, especially when grooming.
3 Incurable biters can be tied up for grooming. Muzzles can be worn.

Kicking

Causes: Boredom as a result of too little work. A spirited nature. Fear, especially in a strange stable or when travelling. Ticklishness. Rats, mice or other animals in the stable.

Remedies:

1 Increase exercise to prevent boredom.
2 Turn out to grass.
3 Handle kindly but firmly; reprimand with voice and slap when horse raises leg.
4 Intruding animals should be eliminated.

5 For incurables, use a box padded with bales of straw or matting or prickly bushes (gorses). In the last resort, attach hobbles to headcollar.

Weaving

When a horse swings head, neck and sometimes forehand from side to side, usually over the stable door, it wastes energy and often loses condition. Weaving is considered an unsoundness.

Causes: Nervousness. Imitation.

Remedies:

1 Exercise and turn out to grass.
2 Attach by length of string two bricks or tyres to top of doorframe so that swaying horse hits one then the other.
3 Various grates can be bought that prevent horse from moving when looking over the top half of the door.

Below: Weaving, a stable vice in which the horse swings from side to side. It can be caused by nervousness and may result in the horse losing healthy condition.

Tearing rugs and bandages
Remedies:
1 Treat cause of itch, if any
2 Put bad-tasting substance on clothing.
3 Hang bib below back of head-collar or muzzle.

Eating bed and droppings
Causes: Boredom. Lack of bulk food. Lack of mineral salts. Worms.
Remedies:
1 Remove cause.
2 Bed on shavings or peat moss.
3 Sprinkle bed with disinfectant.
4 Use a muzzle.
5 Tie horse up before work.

Halter-pulling
Causes: Fear as tightening over the poll felt when pulling back. Realization that he can escape.
Remedies: If frightened either
1 Attach rope to ring of string that breaks when he pulls back, or
2 Stay with tied-up horse to ensure he is not frightened.
3 If he wants to get free, use unbreakable (nylon) halter (headcollar) and rope and tie up tightly

Brushing
When two forelegs or two hind legs brush one another, marks or damage to the fetlock joints or coronet may result.
Causes: Conformation or action. Clenches risen on shoe. Bad shoeing.
Remedies:
1 Correct shoeing and/or use of feather-edged shoes (inner side is built up and has no holes).
2 Use brushing boots and/or Yorkshire boots. Bandages can also be used but they need to be put on by an expert.

Over-reaching
Hind toe/toes hit forelegs, usually on the heel.
Causes: Horse's action results in forelegs not extending enough, or hind legs too much. Galloping and jumping.
Remedies:
1 Treat wound or bruise.

2 Shoe so that hind hoof is wide, square and even concave in front. Clips must be level with hoof.
3 Use over-reach boots.

Crib-biting and windsucking
Crib-biters or cribbers, by gripping objects with their teeth and gulping in air, can damage teeth, making it difficult to eat. Windsuckers suck in air without gripping anything; but sucking air into stomach can cause indigestion and colic. Both habits are considered an unsound-ness.
Causes: Lack of exercise and boredom. Imitation. Irritation of stomach. Lack of bulk food.
Remedies:
1 Plenty of exercise.
2 Constant supply of hay, or a salt lick to keep horse entertained in stable.

Below: Brushing, when the inside of a hoof interferes with the opposite leg, causing cuts and abrasions. It can occur on both hind and forelegs.

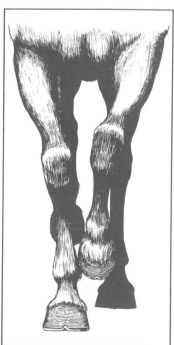

3 Removal of projections that can be gripped with teeth.
4 Muzzle can be worn, except when feeding.
5 Cribbing strap (available from saddlers) can be used.
6 Fluted bit with perforated hollow mouthpiece can be worn; prevents air being sucked in.
7 Paint woodwork with anti-chew mixture (available at saddlers). NB Keep horse away from others, who may copy habits.

Forging
When toe of the hind shoe strikes underneath of the fore shoe.
Causes: Weak young horse. Bad conformation. Feet too long in toe.
Remedies:
1 None necessary for the weak or young horse who will normally just grow out of the habit.
2 Front shoes can be made concave; hind shoes should be set well back under the wall at toe and be squared off. Hind shoe can have thin heels so that the forward action of the hind hooves is restricted.

Above: Crib-biting or cribbing, when a horse grips a surface or object and gulps in air.
Below: Forging, when a rear hoof strikes the toe of a front hoof, making a clicking noise. Young horses affected with this problem usually grow out of the habit.

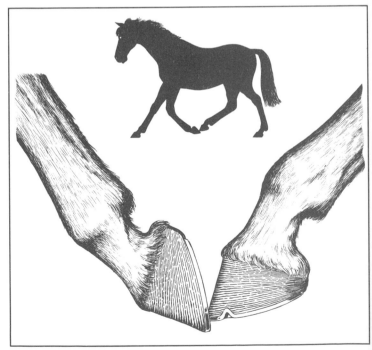

General treatments

Poulticing: Used for bruises, abscesses, swelling and pain. Animalintex or kaolin can be applied in accordance with maker's instructions.

Fomentation: Used for relief of pain and swellings. Cut a piece, approximately 60 × 75cm (24 × 30in) out of towelling or blanket. Fold into four and hold by two corners. Dip into a bucket of warm, salty water (handful of salt to half a bucket of water). Remove, wring and wrap around the injury. Repeat frequently, maintaining temperature by adding hot water to bucket. To test the temperature: before applying to injury, hold back of hand against soaked material and it should be just bearable to keep it there.

Cold treatment: Used for relief of pain and swelling, except in cracked heels and mud fever. Hold a hose pipe over affected area and allow a trickle of water to drop on to the injury.

Cotton wool or gamgee soaked in cold water or lead lotion can then be lightly bandaged on to the injury; renew dressing at regular intervals.

FIRST-AID EQUIPMENT

Items	Use
Veterinary clinical thermometer	
Pair of blunt surgical scissors	
Calico bandages five 5cm (2in) and five 7cm (3in)	
Cotton wool (in small rolls)	
25g (1oz) packets of lint	
Roll of gamgee tissue (gauze bandage)	
Cough expectorant	coughs
Colic drink (from vet)	colic
Lanolin or glycerine	sores (eg, cracked heels)
Antibiotic powder	wounds
Iodine	wounds and fungi
Boracic lotion or ointment	eyes
Animalintex or kaolin	poulticing and reducing inflammation
Lead lotion	sore back
Worming powder	worms
Epsom salts (Magnesium sulphate)	14-85gm (½-3oz) in food or water as a laxative
Methylated spirit	girth galls, etc
Anti-parasitic dressing	ringworm
Cornucrescine	growth of hoof
Dermoline shampoo	skin disorders

Note: Store the above items in a cupboard, box or trunk.

Nature has provided the horse with a tangible calendar — its teeth. Up to the age of eight, the teeth undergo recognizable changes each year, and it is perfectly possible, if you know the signs, to make an accurate assessment of the animal's age. From nine to 18 or so, age is less easy to pinpoint but, allowing for approximately one year's error on either side, it can still be done. Over 20, other indications of age must be sought; and the margin of error is considerable. Because of the difficulty in making a really accurate judgment, horses over the age of eight are often described as 'aged'.

Methods of ageing

The guidelines to age are the six incisors — the tearing teeth — in each jaw at the front of the mouth. In both the lower and the upper jaw they are divided into two centrals, two laterals on either side of the centrals, and two corners on either side of these. The molars — the grinding teeth — at the back may be ignored.

The sets of teeth

The horse has two sets of teeth, deciduous (milk) and permanent. By examining the types of teeth in the mouth, the age of horses up to four and a half years (the age at which the last permanent teeth erupt) can be ascertained. The teeth erupt in order; first the centrals, then the laterals, and finally the corners.

Wear of teeth

The other aid to ageing is the wear of the teeth. Horses' teeth are not enclosed in enamel, and therefore wear down. By examining the wearing surface, known as the table, age can be judged.

The table changes in shape as the tooth — which tapers towards its roots — is worn down. On a new tooth the shape of the table is oval, but with wear it becomes circular and eventually triangular.

The nature of the surface of the table changes too, as continuing wear exposes parts of the tooth closer and closer to its roots. The new tooth has a cavity in its centre called the infundibulum. As the tooth wears, this cavity is flattened and becomes dark as it is filled up with food. A tooth that has a flat table and a dark ring in the centre is said to be 'in wear'. Eventually the tooth is worn down so much that the infundibulum disappears altogether and its dark ring can no longer be seen on the table. Before this occurs, a brown line in front of the infundibulum appears, on the table of the central incisors at first, then on the table of the laterals and corners. It is called the dental star and is part of the substance of the tooth (dentine) that comes to the surface as the tooth wears down.

The profile

When the set of teeth is viewed from the side, in the case of a young horse, the profile is vertical, but as the teeth wear more behind than in front, their profile becomes increasingly horizontal with age.

Stages in the ageing process

At birth, a foal may already possess the two central incisors at top and bottom, or they may appear at any time within the first four weeks. The teeth on either side of the central incisors (the laterals) erupt within two months, and are followed during the next six months by the outside (corner) incisors. Milk teeth are white, fairly small and shell-shaped — that is, they narrow toward the base. Wear is quite noticeable on these teeth by the time the horse is two years old.

Two and a half to six years

At the age of two and a half years, the central incisors drop out and the first permanent teeth appear. These are larger than the milk teeth, have straighter sides and are brownish-yellow in colour. At three and a half to four years the teeth on either side of the central incisors (the laterals) are replaced by second teeth. At about the same time tushes, or canine teeth, will appear in stallions and geldings, although they are usually absent in mares. Between four and a half and five years the last of the milk teeth are lost and new corner incisors grow.

At first the permanent teeth are quite small, with cavities, but they gradually come into wear, and about 18 months after eruption the tables become flattened so that the dark ring of the infundibulum becomes obvious. By the time the horse is six years old, the tables of all the incisors will meet evenly, and show signs of wear. At this stage a horse is said to have a full mouth.

Seven to 15 years
At seven years old, the upper corner incisors sometimes develop a hook, called the 'seven

year hook'. It disappears by the time the horse is eight years old. At seven years the dental star, a brownish line, appears on the tables of the teeth, between the infundibulum and the other edge. It will first be seen on the central incisors, and by the time the horse is nine will be present on the corners.

The next noticeable change in the teeth occurs at about ten years. A slight depression will become apparent near the gum on the outer surface of the upper corner incisors. This feature is known as Galvayne's groove. Over the next few years, it will

The horse jaw (*Below*)
1 Incisors—tearing teeth
2 Molars—grinding teeth

Longitudinal section through an incisor (*Below*)
1 Infundibulum
2 Central enamel
3 Peripheral enamel
4 Cement
5 Dentine
6 Pulp cavity
7 Root

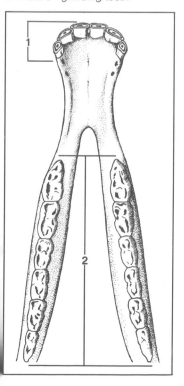

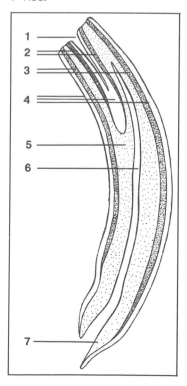

gradually extend down the tooth, reaching a third of the way down when the horse is 13.

During these years the blackish mark, or infundibulum, becomes lighter. It disappears from the central incisors at 12 and from all teeth by 15; the dental star will now be in the centre of each tooth. At the same time the wearing away of the teeth gives them a more triangular shape.

Fifteen to 30 years

From 15 onwards, age assessment is very uncertain. It is based mainly on the length of Galvayne's groove, which should be halfway down the tooth by the time the horse is 15. As Galvayne's groove lengthens, so, too, do the teeth. A 20-year-old horse will have rather long, sloping teeth and quite a pronounced Galvayne's groove. From 25 onwards Galvayne's groove starts to disappear, and by 30 it has gone completely, leaving only dental stars (brown lines).

A horse's life span can be anything from 20 to 40 years, and an aged appearance is not necessarily an indication of the animal's real age. In fact, as with humans, a full and interesting life may well delay the onset of old age. Provided he receives proper care, a horse can continue to lead a useful working existence well into the late 20s or 30s.

Care of teeth

Proper care includes regular

AGEING

Age	Teeth	Table	
Birth—2 years			
1-4 weeks	central incisors erupt	gradually teeth lose cavity and come into wear	
4-8 weeks	lateral incisors erupt	assuming uniform size and appearance	
6-9 months	corner incisors erupt		
2 years	full mouth of deciduous teeth of uniform size		
2-6 years			
2½ years	central incisors erupt		
3½ years	lateral incisors erupt		
4 years		central incisors in wear	oval
4½ years	corner incisors erupt		
5 years		lateral incisors in wear	
6 years		corner incisors in wear	
7-15 years			becoming more circular
7 years	7-year hook in upper corner incisor	dental star in centrals	
8 years		dental star in laterals	
9 years		dental star in corners	
10 years	Galvayne's groove appears		
12 years		infundibulum goes from centrals	becoming more triangular
13 years		infundibulum goes from laterals	
14 years		infundibulum goes from corners	
15 years	Galvayne's groove half way down	infundibulum all gone	
15-30 years			completely triangular
20 years	Galvayne's groove complete	infundibulum all gone and only dental stars (brown line) visible	
25 years	Galvayne's groove half way out		
30 years	Galvayne's groove gone completely		

attention to the teeth. Filing will be necessary from time to time, especially as the horse grows older. An old horse with overlong teeth will have difficulty in eating, and so will be unable to take in sufficient food to cope with the work he has to do. Sharp edges on the teeth can make it painful for a horse to accept the bit when ridden, so check the teeth if any mouthing problems arise.

Signs of old age

An extremely old horse will suffer from a general slowing down of his metabolism. Hollows appear above the eyes, joints may become swollen and rheumatic, and the coat will lose the shine of youth. Dark-coloured horses will show an ever-increasing number of white hairs, particularly in the winter coat and on the face and head.

It is tempting to keep an old favourite until he dies from natural causes, and modern veterinary treatment is so efficient that many an old horse can survive conditions that would have killed him in the past. But though a long and peaceful retirement may seem a fair reward for years of loyal service, old horses may suffer acutely from boredom and loneliness even if they are not in pain. Generally speaking, it is better to have a horse humanely put down rather than allow him to pine away through lack of work and attention and a feeling of uselessness.

	Diagram	
al profile		At 2 years teeth uniform and almost all in wear
al profile		At 4 years temporary teeth lost cavity-in wear permanents (still have cavity) not in wear permanents-in wear
e starts to change from al to horizontal yne's groove ay down		At 10 years infundibulum present in all teeth corners still oval dental stars in all teeth centrals becoming more triangular
singly horizontal		At 15 years all infundibulum gone dental stars visible

THE GAITS OF THE HORSE

The walk
A four-beat gait.
The horse moves one leg after another so that four hoof beats can be heard.

Sequence
1 Left foreleg.
2 Right hind leg.
3 Right foreleg.
4 Left hind leg.
Two or three legs are always on the ground, so there is no moment of suspension. It is a comfortable pace for the rider.

Faults
1 Hoof beats not rhythmical.
2 The four hoof beats not distinct: two-time walk is possible and is a bad fault which needs correcting.
3 Hooves dragged.
4 Horse does not 'track up'; ie, hind legs do not overlap the fores. In a good walk, the hind should be placed further forward than the lateral foreleg just raised.

The gaits of the horse (Below)
1 *Walk—a four-beat gait*
2 *Trot—a two-beat diagonal gait*
3 *Canter—a three-beat gait*

The trot
A two-beat gait known as the jog by Western-style riders.
The horse moves the diagonal hind and forelegs together.

Sequence
1 Left foreleg and right hind leg leave ground.
2 Right foreleg and left hind leg leave ground *before* left fore and right hind touch the ground; therefore, there is a brief moment of suspension.
At the moment when all four legs are suspended in the air, the rider finds it difficult to sit in the saddle. This has led to the development of posting (rising trot), in which the rider puts weight in the stirrups and rises, to sit again when the horse's legs are on the ground.

Faults
1 If trot becomes hurried and forelegs reach the ground before the hinds, four instead of two hoof-beats are heard.
2 Hind legs may be dragged so they reach the ground before forelegs. (Again, this means a four-time pace.)
3 One hind leg moves further under the body than another.

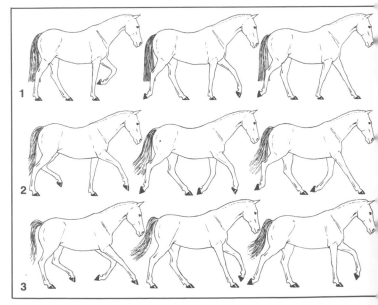

The canter
A three-beat gait known as the lope by Western-style riders. The horse moves in bounds with either the right foreleg or the left foreleg leading.

Sequence of canter to the right
1 Left hind leg on the ground.
2 Right hind leg and left foreleg placed on ground at the same time.
3 Right foreleg placed on ground after left hind leg has risen.
4 All four legs in the air.

Faults
1 Four hoof beats are heard. This occurs when hind leg is put to the ground before corresponding foreleg (2 above); it usually happens when the horse loses impulsion (forward-driving force).
2 A disunited canter. Left leg leads in front, right leg behind, or vice versa.

The gallop
A four-beat gait.
The gallop is an unrestrained canter. The strides are longer and the moment of suspension (stage 4 in sequence) is much longer.

The pace
A two-beat gait.

Sequence
1 Left hind and left foreleg strike ground together.
2 Right hind leg and right foreleg strike the ground. This is not a comfortable pace for the rider.

In America, where the saddle-horse uses five gaits, adaptations of the pace are taught. Particular attention is paid to the animal's head carriage in this riding style.
NB Although these additional gaits come naturally to this breed of horse, training is needed to produce them correctly.

The stepping pace or slow gait
A four-beat gait sequence as for the pace, except that the left foreleg strikes the ground just before the left hind; similarly, right fore before right hind.

The rack
A four-beat gait.
Sequence the same as for the stepping pace but there is a longer interval between the foreleg striking the ground and the hind leg on the same side striking the ground.

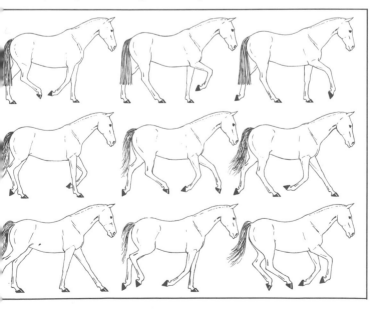

THE HORSE IN LAW AND INSURANCE

Basic law

The law relating to horses is basically simple, although it can be complicated by such factors as the duty of care and contributory negligence. There is a saying that every dog is allowed one bite, which means that, the first time a dog bites anyone, its owner can plead ignorance of the vice. The same applies to horses: the first kick does not constitute breach of the duty to take care on the part of the person in charge of the horse. The second kick does, provided it can be proved that the owner was aware of the previous incident or of the horse's general temperament.

Previous knowledge

There are subtle interpretations to be put on incidents in which previous knowledge is claimed by the injured party. Every horseman knows that a red ribbon tied to a horse's tail indicates that the horse is a kicker—that is to say, a kicker of horses—and injury to any horse it kicked would be the responsibility of its owner. But if, while wearing the red ribbon, it kicked a person or a car, which it had never done before, legal liability would not rest with the owner, although the onus of proving ignorance would fall on him.

Similarly, liability in damages lies with the owner only where a vice, such as kicking or biting, is concerned. Playfulness, at least in law, is not deemed a vice and the owner is not necessarily liable if his horse knocks someone over in play. This is important in relation to a public footpath passing through a field in which horses are kept.

Reason and the law

The law seeks at all times to be reasonable. It would not be reasonable for someone to claim damages if he was bitten by a horse while feeding it with tit-bits over a fence, even if the owner was aware of its tendency to bite. If, however, the land close to the outside of the fence was a public footpath and people passing along the footpath were within reach of the biter, it would be the responsibility of the owner either to see that the horse could not reach the passers-by, or to erect a warning sign that is clearly visible from the footpath.

Straying animals

In the UK the Animals Act of 1971 laid down for the first time that damage caused by straying livestock is the responsibility of the person having possession of the stock. There are a few exceptions, such as straying from a highway that the animal is using lawfully, or from unfenced common land; but, generally speaking, it is up to the owner to see that fences enclosing his horses are strongly built and adequate for their purpose.

In the USA the law is similar and the touchstone in torts (the lawyer's word for civil liability) is 'reasonable standard of care'. That is to say, liability occurs when someone's behaviour falls below what a reasonable and prudent person would or should have done under similar circumstances. Consequently, an owner who leaves a paddock gate unlocked, enabling a horse to break out and cause damage, is liable.

Nevertheless, accidents do happen. Gates are left open or unlatched, and animals have an annoying habit of finding weak spots in hedges before the owner does. This seems invariably to happen at dusk; often the first the owner knows about it is a telephone call or visit from a neighbour. Almost always the horse can be retrieved and the gap closed at a cost of nothing more than a few wasted hours. Perhaps once in 100 such incidents, however, horse and owner find themselves in trouble; there may be damage to a person or car, or a loved horse may be killed or injured; and later, litigation may add further worry and distress.

Contributory negligence
If an incident results in an action being brought, there may be grounds for the defendant to claim contributory negligence on

Below: This spectacular fall underlines the hazards of eventing.

the part of the plaintiff. Patting a confirmed biter when asked not to do so might constitute contributory negligence, as would taunting a horse until it became savage. Sounding a car horn right beside a known kicker of cars could also be held in law to have contributed to the resulting damage.

The acceptance of risk

Knowledge and acceptance of the risks involved could absolve the owner from any liability. Injuries from a fall, in circumstances where falls are possible, would not form the basis of a claim—for example, on a racecourse, or hunting, or in a cross-country event. Similarly, a groom who is kicked and injured, after willingly entering the stable of a horse that is known to kick, cannot claim damages from his employer.

Riding schools and public stables

Anyone who runs a riding school or public stable is deemed to owe a higher standard of care (because of the profit motive) than a person who merely lends a horse without compensation. Although posted notices may disclaim liability for accidents, an establishment cannot contract away gross negligence, such as renting a horse known to be difficult to an obviously inexperienced rider, or failing to inform about dangerous conditions along trails where accidents have previously happened. As a practical matter, insurance will cover most liability, but no school or stable wants to be known as a place where accidents are a frequent occurrence.

A sales contract

In the USA it is becoming more common to use a written sales contract when purchasing a horse. A written agreement is better than a handshake to hold both buyer and seller to all terms and conditions. The method of payment should be spelled out; for example, one half now, and the balance as soon as a chosen veterinarian has certified that the horse is sound and in good health. It is advisable to include any claims made by the seller, as well as the duration of any trial period during which the purchaser may assess the suitability of the horse.

Insurance against liability for damages

The only essential insurance for any horse owner is personal liability coverage. This protects the policy-holder, or anyone riding or driving the animal with the policy-holder's permission, against legal liability for personal injury to, or damage to the property of, third parties, caused by the horse.

The insurance of a horse

The problem of what insurance to take out may be difficult to settle. The owner of a valuable animal does not hesitate: his horse is insured as a matter of course to protect his investment. However much the owner may wince at the premiums, they constitute part of the expected annual cost of maintaining his property, an entry on the expenditure side of his balance sheet as necessary as the price of a ton of hay.

A decision is difficult to reach if the horse concerned has a comparatively low market value. Though a family horse's sentimental worth may be high, the premium for insuring him may represent the cost of several weeks of winter forage, a new bridle or a visit to the farrier. For this reason, many animals live out their lives without ever appearing on an insurance company's books.

The size of the premium depends on:

1 The age of the horse (those over 12 years are more expensive to insure).
2 The use of the horse. A low rate is quoted for hacking, gymkhanas, driving and dressage; a slightly higher rate for show-jumping; still more for eventing, point-to-pointing and hunting; and the highest rate of all for steeplechasing.

The type of cover
1 Death from accident.
2 Death from accident, illness or disease.
3 Death from accident, illness or disease, or loss of use of the horse.

A combination policy
It is possible, however, to take out a combination policy, which covers a number of risks connected with horses and riding. These include: death or humane slaughter resulting from accidental injury or illness (foaling [except in the case of mares over 12 years old having their first foal], fire, lightning and travelling are covered); permanent loss of use; veterinary fees and expenses incurred in foaling and protective inoculations; loss by theft or straying. Riders are insured against death or injury, and the personal liability of the policy-

Above: Eventing is rated as a high risk for insurance purposes. Falls such as this may injure both horse and rider quite badly.

holder is covered. Saddles, bridles and other tack are covered against any accidental loss, damage or theft, provided that they are kept in a private house or in locked premises.

The average premium in the UK for such a policy is about six percent of the sum insured for horses kept for private hacking, showing, gymkhana events, driving, Pony Club events, jumping, polo, hunting, hunter trials and one-day events, or five percent if the last five are excluded. Cover is further limited when horses reach 15 years of age, and are more likely to become unsound. A horse may live anything from 20 to 40 years.

If there is any doubt as to the colour of the coat, then the colour of the points (muzzle, tips of ears, mane and tail and extremities of the four legs) is the deciding factor.

Bay
Brownish colour (shades vary from reddish and yellowish to approaching brown). The points are black.

Black
Coat, limbs, mane and tail are black. Any markings are white.

Brown
Dark brown or nearly black, with brown to black points.

Sorrel (Chestnut)
Ginger, yellow or reddish colour, with similarly coloured mane and tail. The three shades of chestnut are dark, liver and light chestnut.

Dun
Blue dun is a diluted black, with black points, and may or may not have a dorsal band and a withers stripe.
Yellow dun is yellowish on a black skin. Points are normally black and there is often a dorsal band and stripes on withers and limbs.

Cream
Cream-coloured on an unpigmented skin. The eye often has a pinkish appearance.

Grey
Hairs are white and black, on a black skin. There are many shades including flea-bitten grey (dark hairs occurring in tufts) and iron grey (black hairs more numerous)

Roan
A blue roan has a basic colour of black or brown and a sprinkling of white.
A strawberry or chestnut roan has a basic colour of chestnut with a sprinkling of white.

Palomino
Golden colour with flaxen mane and tail.

Pinto or calico
A blotched or spotted pattern.
A piebald has large, irregular patches of black and white.
A skewbald's coat has large patches of white and any colour but black.
An odd coloured horse has a blotched coat which consists of more than two colours.

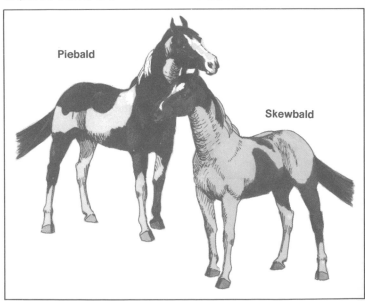

Piebald

Skewbald

Markings are areas of white on the head, body and limbs.

Head

Star is a white mark on the forehead.

Stripe is a narrow white mark down the face.

Blaze is a broad white mark down the face, usually extending from eyes to muzzle.

White face is white forehead, eyes, nose and parts of muzzle.

Snip is a small area of white in the region of the nostrils.

Wall eye is white or blue-white colouring in the eye, due to lack of pigment in the iris.

Legs

Stocking is white on the leg, from coronet to knee or hock.

Sock is white covering the fetlock and part of the cannon region.

Body

Zebra marks are stripes on the limbs, neck, withers or quarters.

Whorls are patterns formed by hairs around a small central spot.

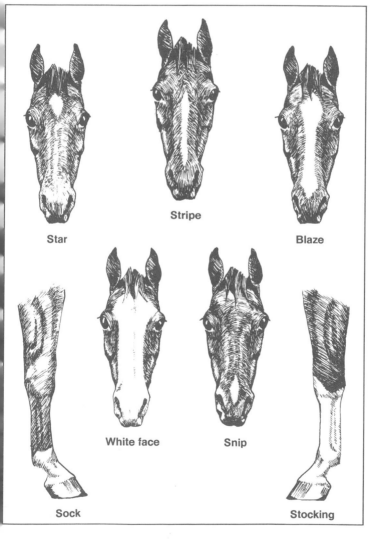

Star

Stripe

Blaze

Sock

White face

Snip

Stocking

	Breed	Usual colour	Average height
Western Europe			
Austria			
Riding horses	Lipizzaner	Grey or bay	15.1hh
Ponies	Haflinger	Chestnut Palomino with flaxen mane and tail	13.3hh
Belgium			
Work horses	Belgian Ardennes	Any	15.3hh
	Brabant or Belgian	Red roan, chestnut	16.2hh
British Isles			
Riding horses	Cleveland Bay	Bay with black points	16hh
	Hackney	Dark brown, black, bay and chestnut	Horse 14.3hh-15.3hh Pony 14.2hh and under
	Welsh Cob	Any except piebald or skewbald	14.3hh
	Thoroughbred	Any whole colour	15.3hh
Work horses	Clydesdale	Bay, brown, white on face and legs	16.hh-17hh
	Shire	Bay and brown. A few are black and grey	16.2hh-17.3hh Can be over 1 to
	Suffolk Punch	Chestnut	16hh About 1 ton
	Irish Draught	Grey, bay, brown, chestnut	Mare 15.1hh Stallion 16.2hh
Ponies	Exmoor	Bay, brown or dun with black points, light mealy muzzle, no white	Stallion 12.3hh Mare 12.2hh
	Dartmoor	Bay, black or brown	Maximum 12.2hh
	New Forest	Any except piebald or skewbald	13.1hh
	Welsh Section A	Any except piebald or skewbald	Maximum 12hh
	Section B	Any except piebald or skewbald	Maximum 13.2hh
	Section C	Any except piebald or skewbald	Maximum 13.2hh
	Section D	Any except piebald or skewbald	14.2hh
	Fell	Black, brown, bay, grey	13.2hh
	Dale	Jet black and dark colours	Up to 14.2hh
	Connemara	Usually grey, but also black, brown, bay	13hh-14hh

Ability and purpose	Features
Intelligent and athletic. Used for High School work, in particular the Spanish Riding School	Originated from Spanish breeds in seventeeth century. Compact body. Largish head
Sure footed. Tough and hardy. General riding, transport, agricultural work	Tyrolese breed produced for mountain work
Lighter type of work horse. Similar to French namesake	Early origins but recently been crossed with other breeds to increase size. Used as a cavalry horse in seventeenth century
Heavy draught work	Originally known as the Flanders Horse. Thick set, stocky, heavily feathered legs. Convex head
Hardy, riding and driving	Short legs, minimum of 9in bone, relatively long back, quarters level
Lively, harness work	Compact body, tail set high, upright feet
Strong, free, forceful action, great presence and zest. Riding and driving	Strong shoulders, silky feathers on legs
Fast, athletic. Racing and competition riding	Developed in seventeenth century from imported Oriental stock. Now the most valuable breed in the world
Lively, active, free elastic action	Long pasterns, long arched neck, great quality, feather on legs
Docile, can be worked at 3 years	Wide chest, white markings, heavy feathers
Long life span, economical feeder, stamina	Square body, massive neck, no feathers, except tuft on fetlock
Good jumpers	No feathers, good shoulders
Very strong. Riding	Prominent 'toad' eyes, deep wide chest, clean legs. Winter coat thick with no bloom
Long life. Riding. Draught work	Head small and fine, strong shoulders, back and loins, full mane and tail
Riding	Short coupled
Riding	
Excellent riding pony	Head tapering to muzzle, long neck, sloping shoulder, great quality
Sturdy, active and strong. Driving	Great substance. Silk feather on legs. Cob type
Sturdy, active and strong. Driving and riding	Great substance. Silk feather on legs
Strength, stamina. Riding, light draught work	Great substance, minimum of 8in bone, fine hair on heels and long curly mane and tail
Strength, docility. Riding and transport	Fine hair on heels, shoulders relatively straight, powerful hinds
Riding	Compact, short-legged

BREEDS OF THE WORLD

	Breed	Usual colour	Average height
British Isles continued			
	Highland a) mainland	Black, brown, varying to dun and grey	14.2hh
	b) islands	Has dark eel stripe along back	As small as 12.2hh
	Shetland	Foundation colour black but now found in all colours	10.2hh
Denmark Riding horses	Danish sports-horse	Any	16hh
	Fredericksborg	Chestnut	16hh
	Knabstrup	Spotted horse	15.3hh
Work horses	Jutland	Black, brown, chestnut	15.3hh
Finland Work horses	Finnish	Chestnut, bay	15.2hh
France Riding horses	Anglo Arab	Any	16hh
	French Trotter	Any	16hh
	Selle Français	Any	16hh
Work horses	Ardennes	Roan, iron grey, bay	16hh
	Boulonnais	Grey	16.2hh
	Breton	Chestnut, grey, roan	16hh
	Percheron	Grey, black	16.1hh
Ponies	Basque	Most	13hh
	Camargue	Grey	14.0hh
	Landais	Most	13.2hh
Germany Riding horses	Bavarian	Any	16hh

Ability and purpose	Features
Riding and light draught work	Broad, short coupled, straight, silky feather on legs, much bone
Independent and headstrong, so needs firm handling. Riding	Double coat in winter, smooth in summer, short back, deep girth, sloping shoulders
General riding and competitions	New breed formed by crossing imported riding horses (Hanoverian etc) with own stock
Driving	Breed nearly died out and outcrosses made with Oldenburgs and East Friesians
Circus work and driving	Lighter but similar to Fredericksborg
Agricultural work	Compact, short legs with feather
General purpose. Transport, military and trotting. Draught work, forestry	Created by crossing Finnish Universal with Finnish Draught stock
Free paces. Racing, jumping, dressage and general riding	Based on crosses between Oriental breeds in South West France and Thoroughbred, or pure Arab and Thoroughbred
High action. Used for riding and competitions but main purpose is trotting races	Crosses between British Trotter and Thoroughbred, and Anglo Normans led to production of the breed in the early nineteenth century
Athletic. All forms of equitation	Regional breeds (notably Anglo Norman), all of which were based on crosses between local work mares and purebreds, were amalgamated under one stud book — Selle Français — in 1964
Sober temperament. Draught work	Originating from the same mountains as their Belgian namesakes, they have very early origins. Flat rectangular head with short light feathered legs
Draught work	Arab ancestors. Elegant for their size. Clean legs
Adaptive and energetic. Draught work	Compact bodies. Short legs, which are almost clean
Stamina. Active. Draught work	Bred by farmers in Le Perche last century. Now one of the most popular work horses in the world. Relatively small fine head. Well proportioned. Clean legs
Quick to mature. Used in mines and for riding	Still roams wild in Pyrenees and Atlantic cantons. Origins unknown but thought to be very ancient as it resembles primitive ponies
Most run wild. Some tamed for herding bulls	Barb origins. Large head
Riding and driving	Elegant, strong. Arab-like head
Riding and agricultural work	Similar development to that of the Württemburg

BREEDS OF THE WORLD

	Breed	Usual colour	Average height
Germany continued			
	Hanoverian	Any	16.1hh
	Hessian Rheinlander Pfalz	Any	16hh
	Holstein	Any	16.1hh
	Oldenburg	Brown, bay, black	16.2hh
	Trakehner	Any	16.1hh
	Westphalian	Any	16.1hh
	Württemburg	Brown, bay, chestnut, black	16hh
Work horses	Noriker/South German Cold-Blood	Bay, brown, chestnut, spotted	16.1hh
	Rhineland Heavy Draught	Sorrel, chestnut, roan	16.2hh
	Schleswig	Chestnut	15.3hh
The Netherlands			
Riding horses	Gelderland	Chestnut, grey	16hh
Work horses	Dutch Draught	Dun, grey, sorrel	16.1hh
	Friesian	Black	15hh
	Groningen	Black, brown	15.3hh
Norway			
Riding horses	Döle Trotter	Black, brown	15hh
Work horses	Döle Horse	Black, brown	15hh
Ponies	Fjord	Dun with dorsal stripe	14hh
Portugal			
Riding horses	Alter-Real	Chestnut, bay, piebald	15.1hh
	Lusitano	Any	15hh
Ponies	Garrano/Minho	Chestnut	11hh
Spain			
Riding horses	Andalusian	Grey, black	15.3hh

Ability and purpose	Features
Very powerful with extravagant action. Riding and driving	Originally a famous carriage horse but crossed with Arab and Thoroughbred to refine. It is the most successful and numerous breed of riding horse in Germany
General riding	Similar types of horses all bred around the Rhine; but each has own stud book
Strong horses. General riding and competitions	Breeding dates from 1300 when used as war horse. Oriental then Cleveland Bay and today the Thoroughbred used to upgrade
Driving and riding	This is the heaviest of the German riding horses
Good action. Competition work and general riding	Refugees in West Germany, originally bred at stud at Trakehnen in East Prussia, which was founded by Frederick William I of Prussia in 1732. Elegant horses
General riding, competitions and driving	Developed largely from Hanoverian strains and is very similar to them
Riding and agricultural work	The central stud is at Marbach where they have been developed by crossing many German breeds
Agricultural work. Transport especially in mountains	Originally bred in Noricum by Romans. Heavy head on short neck
Powerful. Heavy draught work	Heavily crested neck. Low to ground. Feathered legs
Driving and agricultural work	Similar to Jutland Cob type
Active type. General riding and competitions. Driving	Originated by crossing native stock in Gelderland with Trotters, Thoroughbreds and Anglo Normans
Docile. One of the most massive of the draught horses	Breed started mid-way through last century
Very active	This breed is old and was popular in medieval times. Particularly compact
Docile. Heavyweight saddle horse. Driving	Strong back and stylish action
Trotting	Lighter version of Döle Horse
Riding and agricultural work	Short feathered legs with very thick mane and tail
Agricultural work and riding	Resembles horses of Ice Age. Upright mane
Extravagant action. Energetic. Famous as High School horses	Originated from Andalusians in eighteenth century. Bred in Alentejo Province
Riding and light agricultural	Fine head with full low-set tail
Hardy light build. Pack ponies, trotting races	Arab ancestry
Intelligent. Attractive action made them popular High School horses in Europe	Barb origins. Still has this breed's flat, almost convex head

BREEDS OF THE WORLD

	Breed	Usual colour	Average height
Sweden Riding horses	Swedish warm-blood	Any	15.3hh
Switzerland Riding horses	Einseidler	Any	15.3hh
	Swiss warm-blood	Any	16hh
Work horses	Freiberger	Blue roan, grey	15.3hh
Eastern Europe			
Czechoslovakia Riding horses	Kladruber	Originally black or grey	16.2hh
Hungary Riding horses	Furioso	Black, brown	16hh
	Nonius	Black, brown	Large over 15.3hh. Small under 15.3hh
Work horses	Murakosi	Chestnut, bay, black	16hh
Poland Riding horses	Malopolski	Any	15.3hh
	Wielkopolski	Any	16hh
Ponies	Konik	Yellow, grey, blue, dun	13hh
	Tarpan	Brown, dun with dorsal stripe	12.1hh
USSR More than 40 recognized breeds but following most well known.			
Riding horses	Akhal-Teke	Any but with character-istic golden sheen	15.1hh
	Budjonny	Chestnut, bay	15.3hh
	Don	Chestnut, grey	15.3hh
	Kabardin	Bay, black	15hh
	Karabair	Bay, grey, chestnut	15.1hh
	Lokai	Any	14.3hh

Ability and purpose	Features
Intelligent. Free paces. General riding. Good competition results	Originated from systematic crossing of native stock with Thoroughbred and German riding horses
Used by military, for riding and transport	Bred for centuries at Einseidler
Good action and temperament. General riding and competitions	New breed created by crossing imported French, Swedish, German and home bred riding horses, and Thoroughbreds
Stamina. Light agricultural work. Transport	Compact strong horse
Riding, driving and light agricultural work	Originated from Spanish breeds. Typically has a long straight back
General riding and driving	Originated in nineteenth century from crosses between Thoroughbred Trotters and native mares
Reliable, active with long stride. General riding and agricultural work	The Anglo Norman was influential in development of the breed. Has an impressive head with long neck
High quality draught horse	Developed this century from crossing Ardennes, Oriental and local breeds
Lighter than Wielkopolski and used mainly for riding	Originated from crosses between local mares, Arabs and Anglo Arabs
Dual purpose, used for general riding and driving	Breed formed by merging older breeds of Masuren and Poznan
Hardy with great vitality. Valuable work ponies	Konik — meaning small horse — is used to cover other types with own names ie Zmudzin, Hucul and Bilgoraj
	Primitive wild horse of northern Europe that vanished. By selective crossing of Przewalski stallions and Konik mares the breed is said to have been re-established
Desert horse, able to withstand great heat and lack of water. Racing, competitions and general riding	Elegant, refined horse bred in Turkemenia. Skeletons of similar fine boned horses found dating back 2,500 years
Good temperament with substance. Riding, competitions and racing	Created this century by crossing Thoroughbreds with Dons
Great stamina. Harness work, general riding, long distance racing	Used by Don cossacks in eighteenth century
Sure footed, good pack horse, especially able in mountains. General riding	Developed by crossing mountain breeds with southern breeds
Great stamina. Dual purpose, used for riding and driving	Bred in Uzbekistan for about 2,400 years
Powerful. Used as pack horse or for general riding, especially in highlands	Originated in seventeenth century in Tadjikistan and have Arab and Karabair ancestors

BREEDS OF THE WORLD

	Breed	Usual colour	Average height
USSR continued			
	Novokirghiz	Dark colours	15hh
	Orlov Trotter	Grey, black	15.3hh but up to 17hh
	Russian Trotter (Metis)	Any	15.3hh
	Tersk	Grey	15.1hh
Ponies	Karabakh	Chestnut, bay, dun with metallic sheen	14.1hh
	Kazakh	Bay and most others	14hh
	Yakut	Greyish, mousy	13hh
Work horses	Latvian	Bay, black, chestnut	16hh
	Russian Heavy	Chestnut	14.3hh
	Soviet Heavy Draught	Any	15.3hh
	Toric	Any	15.1hh
	Vladimir Heavy Draught	Chestnut, bay, roan	15.3hh
Turkey			
Riding horses	Karacabey	Solid colours	15.3hh
Iran			
Riding horses	PlateauPersian	Solid colours	15.0hh
	Turkoman	Any	15.2hh
Yemen			
Riding horses	Arab	Originally bay and chestnut, grey is now common	15hh
Morocco & Algeria			
Riding horses	Barb	Bay, brown, chestnut, grey	14.3hh
South Africa			
Ponies	Basuto	Chestnut, bay	14.2hh

Ability and purpose	Features
General riding—especially good in high altitudes and for herding stock	Improved by crossing Kirghiz, which was smaller, with Don and Thoroughbred
Harness work and trotting races	Developed in 1770s by Count Orlov who crossed Arab, Thoroughbred, Dutch, Mecklenburg and Danish horses
Trotting races	Developed by crossing American Standardbred and Orlov when former became faster than latter. Faster but not so handsome as Orlov
Good temperament. Used for general riding, circus and dressage work	Originated from Strelets breed—Arabians that nearly died out after World War I. Outside Arabians and their cross breeds used. Larger than pure bred Arabs
Lively mountain horse used for riding and racing	Originated in Karabakh in Trans-Caucasian uplands and has Arab ancestors
Tough, able to withstand steppe life. Herding cattle, long distance riding, especially in highlands	Originated as horses of nomads in Kazakhstan. Today are being crossed with Don to produce larger version— the Kustanair
Used for riding, pack work, transport, harness	Long hairy coats. Survive in Yakut territory (beyond Polar circle)
Great pulling strength—draught horses	These extremely powerful work horses are bred in Baltic states by crossing local Zhmuds with larger imports—Finnish Draught and Swedish Ardennes
Lively, fast gaits	Founded in Ukraine where local breeds were crossed with Ardennes, Percherons and Orlov Trotters
Active and relatively fast. The most popular heavy horse in USSR	Developed by crossing local breeds with Belgians, Ardennes, and Percherons. Not so massive as European heavy horses
Agricultural work and in harness	Originated by crossing Hackney and East Friesian with local Estonian breeds
Strong puller, energetic. Agricultural work	Created in nineteenth century by crossing local horses with Clydesdale and Shire
Riding and harness work	Developed from native horses crossed with Nonius from Hungary
Strong, sure footed. Riding	Amalgamation of plateau breeds
Floating action. Long-distance racing, endurance rides, and general riding	Originated, like the Akhal-Teké, from the Turkemene horse
Light, graceful action; fast, with great stamina. General riding and racing	Origins vague but thought to have roamed wild in Yemen until tamed c. 3000BC. Oldest pure breed and has had great influence on all other breeds. Typically has a concave head; croup level with the back
Fast. Used for general riding	An old breed with Arab blood. Typically has the tail set lower than Arab. Convex ram-shaped head
Riding and general transport	Thick set and long in the back. Originated from Arab and Barb stock

BREEDS OF THE WORLD

	Breed	Usual colour	Average height
Australia			
Riding horses	Australian Stock Horse	Any	16hh
Ponies	Australian pony	Any	13hh
South America			
Argentina			
Riding horses	Criollo	Dun, sorrel, palomino	14.3hh
Brazil			
Riding horses	Crioulo	Dun, sorrel, palomino	14.2hh
	Mangalarga	Grey, sorrel, roan	15.3hh
Peru			
Riding horses	Peruvian Stepping Horse	Dun, sorrel, palomino	14hh
Venezuela			
Riding horses	Llanero	Light colours, pinto, with dark mane and tail	14hh
North America			
Riding horses	Appaloosa	White coat with black or brown spots	15.1hh
	Mustang	Any	14.2hh
	Morgan	Any	15hh
	Quarter-horse	Any	15hh
	Palomino	Golden with light mane and tail	Any
	Pinto	White splashes on black (piebald) or on other colours (skewbald)	Various
	Saddle-bred	Any	15.2hh
	Standard-bred	Any	15.3hh
	Tennessee Walking Horse	Any	15.2hh
Ponies	Pony of Americas	Any	13hh

Ability and purpose	Features
Riding, herding	Originated by crossing Arab, Anglo Arab and Thoroughbred with local stock in last century. Became known as the Waler
General riding	Foundation stock was Welsh
Great stamina. Used for endurance work and for general riding	Short head, stocky. Originated from Andalusians, imported in sixteenth century, which ran wild on the pampas
General riding and herding	Similar background to Criollo but original stock mainly Alters from Portugal
General and long-distance riding and harness work	Originated from Crioulo crossed with imports from Spain and Portugal. Also selective breeding of Mangalarga has produced a heavier breed—the Campolino
Especially smooth gaits; the amble (a pace) enables the rider to cover great distances at speed and in comfort	Developed, like Criollos, from Spanish and Portuguese horses that ran wild
Great stamina; used for endurance riding	Smaller and finer than other Criollos but from similar origins
Used by Indians who took advantage of camouflage colouring. Now popular for Western riding	Developed by Nez Percé Indians in Palouse, Idaho
Sturdy. Riding, showing, stock	Spanish origins. Ran wild
Short active stride; great stamina. Very versatile, used for riding and harness work	Originated in New England from the Justin Morgan Horse (1789). Particularly short in the back and legs
Sure footed with great acceleration; excellent ranch horses. Racing, rodeo work, polo and general riding	Developed as quarter-mile sprinters. Foundation sire was the Thoroughbred 'Janus'. Largest stud book in the world. Stocky with powerful hindquarters
All types of use	Not yet an established breed as not yet breeding true to type but stud book now exists for which horses qualify through colour
Tough. Used by Indians. General riding horse	Not a true breed. Defined by colour like palominos
High action; either 3-gaited, when mane is roached, or 5-gaited. Riding and driving	Short back, long tapering neck. Foundation stock was Thoroughbred and Arab
Tough. Can trot nearly as fast as Thoroughbred can gallop. Some pace rather than trot when they move lateral rather than diagonal pairs	Foundation sire was the Thoroughbred 'Messenger' imported from UK in 1795. Strong hindquarters and long back
Comfortable paces. High-stepping gaits with fast running walk. General riding and driving	Developed as hacks for plantation owners in nineteenth century from a mixture of US breeds
Riding	New breed developed by crossing Quarter-horse, Arab and Appaloosa

INDEX

Page numbers in **bold type** refer to main text entries, including any illustration captions on that page; numbers in Roman type to other text entries; *italic* numbers to captions.

Picture Credits

The Publishers wish to thank the following photographers and agencies who have supplied photographs for this book. Photographs have been credited by page number and position on the page: (B) Bottom, (T) Top, etc.

Animal Photography Ltd: Half title page, 41, 48, 53, 62
Eric Crichton: 6
Anne Cumbers: 56-7, 58, 59, 113
Findlay Davidson: 73
Marc Henrie: 69, 150
Roger Hyde (© Salamander Books

Ltd.): 42, 55, 76, 143, 145(T)
Jane Kidd: 60-61, 74-5, 148-49
E.D. Lacey: 26, 52, 66, 84-5, 91, 95, 96-7, 134, 179, 181
Picturepoint: Contents page
W. Rentsch: 14, 15
Mike Roberts: Endpapers, 100-101
Bruce Scott (© Salamander Books Ltd.): 7-11, 13, 16-18, 20, 21, 23, 25, 28, 30-36, 38, 39, 54, 92, 93, 108-9, 110-111, 116-120, 124, 135, 136-37, 138-39
M. Stannard: 103
Tony Stone: Title page